THE MOLLUSC

an Edwardian Comedy

BY

HUBERT HENRY DAVIES

Afterword by Hugh Walpole

VERTVOLTA PRESS
REDISCOVERY EDITION

*'The Mollusc' by Hubert Henry Davies,
was originally originally produced
at the Criterion Theatre London October, 1907.*

Reprint & redesign Copyright © 2014, 2019
by Vertvolta Press.

All rights reserved. Published in the United States
by Vertvolta Press.
No part of this book's design may be reproduced in any manner whatsoever without prior written permission.

Book and Cover Design: Vladimir Verano

Cover Image: © 2019 Vladimir Verano

ISBN: 978-1-60944-098-5

Published in the United States by

VERTVOLTA PRESS
3614 CALIFORNIA AVE SW #236
SEATTLE, WA 98116

vvdesignpress@gmail.com

vertvoltapress.com

Outsiders Inn's Production of 'The Mollusc'

November 7, 8, 9 & 14, 15, 16 2014
PURLIEU HALL, Seattle, Washington

Directed by Gregory Berry

Assistant Director - Sofia Rybin

Starring:

TOM KEMP - Brandon Brown
Miss ROBERTS - Rose Kinne
MR. BAXTER - Patrick J. Lucey-Conklin
MRS. BAXTER - Erin Reitz

Lighting Design - David Verkade
Costume/Stage Design - Anna Curtiss
Produced by - Sofia Rybin & Gregory Berry
Poster Design, Graphic Design - Vladimir Verano

CONTENTS

Act I 1

Act II 47

Act III 103

Afterword 139

The Mollusc

The First Act

SCENE. MRS. BAXTER'S *sitting-room. A pleasant, well-furnished room. French windows open to the garden, showing flower-beds in full bloom, it being summer time. As the audience looks at the stage there is a door on the left hand side at the back, and from the door a few stairs lead down to the room. Nearer and also on this side is a fireplace. Against this same wall is a flower pot on a table containing a plant in bloom. There is plenty of comfortable furniture about the room.*

It is evening after dinner. Lamps are lighted and the windows closed. MR. BAXTER, *a man about forty, is seated near a lamp reading "Scribner's Magazine." The door opens and* MISS ROBERTS *comes in. She is a pretty, honest-looking English girl about twenty-four. She comes towards* MR. BAXTER.

Act I

Miss ROBERTS.

Mr. Baxter—are you very busy?

MR. BAXTER.

No, Miss Roberts.

Miss ROBERTS.

I want to speak to you.

MR. BAXTER.

Yes. Won't you sit down?

Miss ROBERTS.

Thank you. [*She does so.*] We shall soon be beginning the summer holidays, and I think after this term you had better have another governess for the girls.

MR. BAXTER.

You want to leave us?

Miss ROBERTS.

I don't *want* to. I shall be very sorry indeed to go. You and Mrs. Baxter have always been so kind to me. You never treated me like a governess.

MR. BAXTER.

You have been with us so long. We have come to look on you as one of the family.

Miss ROBERTS.

I can't tell you how often I have felt grateful. I don't want to leave you at all, and it will almost break my heart to say good-bye to the children, but I *must* go.

Act I ❊

MR. BAXTER.

[*Anxiously.*] You are not going to be married?

Miss ROBERTS.

[*Smiling.*] Oh, no—nothing so interesting—I'm sorry to say.

MR. BAXTER.

Have you told my wife you think of leaving?

Miss ROBERTS.

[*Slightly troubled.*] I began to tell Mrs. Baxter several times; at the beginning of the term and three or four times since—but she was always too busy or too tired to attend to me; each time she asked me to tell her some other time—until I don't quite know what to do. That's why I've come to *you*.

MR. BAXTER.

[*Slightly disconcerted.*] But it's not my place to accept your notice.

Miss ROBERTS.

I know—but if I might explain to you—

MR. BAXTER.

Certainly.

Miss ROBERTS.

It's this. I can't teach the girls anything more. Gladys is nearly twelve and Margery, though she is only nine, is very bright; she often asks me the most puzzling questions—and the truth is—I have not had a good enough education myself to take them any further.

Act I

MR. BAXTER.

Aren't they rather young to go to school?

Miss ROBERTS.

I think you need a governess with a college education, or, at any rate, some one who doesn't get all at sea in algebra and Latin.

MR. BAXTER.

I should have thought you might read and study.

Miss ROBERTS.

I used to think so—but I find I haven't the time.

MR. BAXTER.

[*Thoughtfully.*] Too much is expected of you besides your duties as the children's governess. I've noticed that—but I don't quite see how I can interfere.

Miss ROBERTS.

Please don't trouble, and don't think I'm complaining. I am always glad to be of use to Mrs. Baxter. It's not for my own sake I want a change; it's for the girls. This is their most receptive age. What they are taught, and *how* they are taught *now*, will mean so much to them later on. I can't bear to think they may suffer all their lives through *my* ignorance.

MR. BAXTER.

[*Politely.*] Oh—I'm sure—

Act I

MISS ROBERTS.

It's very kind of you to say so—but I know what it is. I have suffered myself for want of a thorough education. Of course I had the ordinary kind, but I was never brought up to know or do anything special. I found myself at a great disadvantage when I had to turn to, and earn my own living.

MR. BAXTER.

Gladys and Margery won't have to earn their own livings.

MISS ROBERTS.

No one used to think that I should have to earn mine—till one day—I found myself alone and poor—after the shipwreck—when my father and mother—and my sister— [*She turns her head away to hide her emotion from* MR. BAXTER.]

MR. BAXTER.

[*Kindly.*] We shall all miss you very much when you go. [*Leaning towards her.*] I shall miss you very much. [*She nods.*] We've had such good walks and talks and games of chess.

MISS ROBERTS

[*Brightly.*] Yes! I've enjoyed them all.

MR. BAXTER.

I hope you have a nice place to go to.

Act I

Miss ROBERTS.

[*Simply.*] I haven't any place to go to. I hoped Mrs. Baxter would help me find a new situation. I can't get one very well without her help, as this is the only place where I have ever been a governess, and after being here four years— [smiles] I must ask Mrs. Baxter to give me a good character.

MR. BAXTER.

[*Meditatively.*] Four years—it doesn't seem like four years. I don't know—though in some ways it seems as if you had always been here. [*Looking at* Miss ROBERTS.] It is very honest of you to give up a good situation for a conscientious reason like this.

Miss ROBERTS.

I don't know.

MR. BAXTER.

[*As an afterthought.*] I suppose it really is your reason for leaving?

Miss ROBERTS.

[*Laughing.*] It's not very nice of you to compliment me on my honesty one minute and doubt it the next.

MR. BAXTER.

[*Seriously.*] No, Miss Roberts, no. I don't doubt it. I was only wondering. I thought perhaps there might be some other reason why you find it difficult to live here—why you think it would be wiser not to stay—

Miss ROBERTS.

[*Innocently.*] No—

MR. BAXTER

I see. Well—as I leave everything to do with the girls' education to Mrs. Baxter—perhaps you will tell *her*. Tell her what you have told *me*.

Miss ROBERTS.

And will you sit in the room?

MR. BAXTER.

Why? What is going to be the difficulty?

Miss ROBERTS.

[*Embarrassed.*] I can't explain very well to you—but if you wouldn't mind sitting in the room. [*She rises.*] I think I hear Mrs. Baxter coming.

[MRS. BAXTER *enters. She is a pretty woman about thirty-five, vague in her movements and manner of speaking. She comes down the room as she speaks.*]

MRS. BAXTER.

I've been wondering where *Scribner's Magazine* is.

MR. BAXTER.

I have it. Have you been looking for it?

MRS. BAXTER.

No—not looking—only wondering.

MR. BAXTER.

Do you want it?

Act I

MRS. BAXTER.

[*Pleasantly.*] Not if you are reading it—though I was just half-way through a story.

MR. BAXTER.

Do take it.

MRS. BAXTER.

[*Taking magazine.*] Don't you really want it?

[*She looks about, selecting the most comfortable chair.*]

MR. BAXTER

It doesn't matter.

MRS. BAXTER.

[*Smiling.*] Thank you. [*She sits.*] Oh, Miss Roberts, I wonder if you could get me the cushion out of that chair? [*Pointing to a chair near a window.*]

Miss ROBERTS.

Certainly. [*She brings the cushion to* MRS. BAXTER *and places it behind her back.*]

MRS. BAXTER.

[*Settling herself.*] Thank you. Now I'm quite comfortable—unless I had a footstool.

Miss ROBERTS.

A footstool? [*She gets a footstool, brings it to* MRS. BAXTER *and places it under her feet.*]

MRS. BAXTER.

[*Without an attempt to move while* Miss ROBERTS *is doing this.*] Don't trouble, Miss Roberts. I didn't mean *you* to do that. *I* could have done it. [*When* Miss ROBERTS *has placed the footstool.*] Oh, how kind of you, but you ought not to wait on me like this. [*Smiles sweetly.*] The paper-knife, please. Who knows where it is? [Miss ROBERTS *takes the paper-knife from* MR. BAXTER *and gives it to* MRS. BAXTER. *To* MR. BAXTER.] I didn't see you were using it, dear, or I wouldn't have asked for it. [*To* Miss ROBERTS.] As you're doing nothing, would you mind cutting some of these pages? I find there are still a few uncut. [*She gives the magazine and paper-knife to* Miss ROBERTS, *then says smiling sweetly.*] Your fingers are so much cleverer than mine. [Miss ROBERTS *begins cutting the magazine.* MRS. BAXTER *leans back comfortably in her chair and says to* MR. BAXTER.] Why don't you get something to do?

MR. BAXTER.

[*Rising.*] I'm going to my room to have a smoke.

[Miss ROBERTS *puts the magazine on the table and goes to* MR. BAXTER *with the paper-knife in her hand.*]

MISS ROBERTS.

No, Mr. Baxter, please, I want you to help me out. I want you to stay while I tell Mrs. Baxter.

MRS. BAXTER.

What's all this mystery? [*Seriously.*] Take care you don't snap that paper-knife in two, Miss Roberts.

Act I

[MR. BAXTER *sits down again.*]

MISS ROBERTS.
[*To* MRS. BAXTER.] I was telling Mr. Baxter before you came into the room—

MRS. BAXTER.
[*Holding out her hand.*] Give me the paper-knife.

[Miss ROBERTS *gives her the paper-knife, which she examines carefully.*]

MISS ROBERTS.
I told you at the beginning of the term, and several times since—

MRS. BAXTER.
It would have been a pity if that paper-knife had been snapped in two. [*She looks up pleasantly at* Miss ROBERTS.] Yes, Miss Roberts?

MISS ROBERTS.
I was saying that I thought—

[MRS. BAXTER *drops the paper-knife accidentally on the floor.*]

MRS. BAXTER.
Oh, don't trouble to pick it up. [Miss ROBERTS *picks up the paper-knife and holds it in her hand.*] Oh, thank you, I didn't mean you to do that.

MISS ROBERTS.
I was saying—

MRS. BAXTER

It isn't chipped, is it?

Miss ROBERTS.

[*Nearly losing her temper.*] No.

[*She marches to the table and lays the paper-knife down.*]

MRS. BAXTER.

It would have been a pity if that paper-knife had been chipped.

Miss ROBERTS.

[*Facing* MRS. BAXTER *with determination, and speaking fast and loud.*] I said I must leave at the end of the term.

MRS. BAXTER.

[*Blandly.*] Aren't you happy with us, Miss Roberts?

Miss ROBERTS.

Oh, yes, thank you. Very.

MRS. BAXTER.

Really happy, I mean.

MR. BAXTER.

Miss Roberts feels that Gladys and Margery are getting too old for her to teach.

Miss ROBERTS.

[*Glancing her gratitude to* MR. BAXTER *for helping her.*] Yes. [*To* MRS. BAXTER.] I've taught them all I know; they need some one cleverer; there ought to be a change.

MRS. BAXTER.
I think you do very nicely.

Miss ROBERTS.
You don't know how ignorant I am.

MRS. BAXTER.
[*Sweetly.*] You do yourself an injustice, dear Miss Roberts.

[Miss ROBERTS *turns appealingly to* MR. BAXTER.]

MR. BAXTER.
It was the algebra, I think you said, Miss Roberts, that you found so especially difficult?

Miss ROBERTS.
Yes. I've no head for algebra,

MRS. BAXTER.
[*Cheerfully.*] Neither have I, but I don't consider myself a less useful woman for that.

Miss ROBERTS.
You're not a governess.

MRS. BAXTER.
Who said I was? Don't let us wander from the point, Miss Roberts.

[Miss ROBERTS *looks appealingly at* MR. BAXTER *again.*]

MR. BAXTER.
The Latin—

Act I

MISS ROBERTS.

Yes, I give myself a lesson at night to pass on to them in the morning—that's no way to do, just keeping a length ahead.

MRS. BAXTER.

Perhaps Mr. Baxter will help you with the Latin. Ask him.

MISS ROBERTS.

I'm afraid even that—

MRS. BAXTER.

Mr. Baxter's a very good Latin scholar. [*Smiling at* MR. BAXTER.] Aren't you, dear?

MR. BAXTER.

[*Reluctantly.*] I read Virgil at school. I haven't looked at him since. After a time one's Latin gets rusty.

MRS. BAXTER.

[*Cheerfully.*] Rub it up. We might begin now, while you're doing nothing. Ask Miss Roberts to bring you the books.

MR. BAXTER.

Oh, no, dear.

MRS. BAXTER.

Why shouldn't we improve our minds?

[*She leans her head back on the cushions.*]

MR. BAXTER.

Not after dinner. [*To* Miss ROBERTS.] I don't see why you want to teach the girls Latin.

Miss ROBERTS.

Mrs. Baxter said she wished them to have a smattering of the dead languages.

MRS. BAXTER.

[*Complacently.*] I learnt Latin. I remember so well standing up in class and reciting "Hic—haec—hoc"—accusative "—hinc—honc—huc."

MR. BAXTER.

[*Correcting her.*] Hoc.

MRS. BAXTER.

Huc, my dear, in *my* book. And the ablative was hibus.

MR. BAXTER.

Hibus!

[MR. BAXTER *and* Miss ROBERTS *both laugh.*]

MRS. BAXTER.

[*Making wild serious guesses.*] Hobibus—no, wait a minute—that's wrong—don't tell me. [*She closes her eyes and murmurs.*] Ablative—ho—hi—hu—no; it's gone. [*She opens her eyes and says cheerfully.*] Never mind. [*To* Miss ROBERTS.] What were we talking about?

Miss ROBERTS.

My ignorance of Latin.

Act I ❂

MRS. BAXTER.

I can't say that *my knowledge* of it has ever been of much service to me. I think Mr. Baxter is quite right. Why teach the girls Latin? Suppose we drop it from the curriculum and take up something else on Latin mornings—

Miss ROBERTS.

[*Earnestly to* MRS. BAXTER.] I wonder if you realize how much all this means to the girls? Their future is so important.

MRS. BAXTER.

[*With the idea of putting* Miss ROBERTS *in her place.*] Of course it is important, Miss Roberts. It is not necessary to tell a mother how important her girls' future is—but I don't suppose we need settle it this evening. [*Wishing to put an end to the discussion, she rises, walks towards the table on which stands the flower pot and says amiably.*] How pretty these flowers look growing in this pot.

Miss ROBERTS.

Would you rather we discussed it tomorrow, Mrs. Baxter?

MRS. BAXTER.

Tomorrow will be my brother's first day here, and he will have so much to tell me after his long absence. I don't think tomorrow would be a good day.

Miss ROBERTS.

The day after?

Act I

MRS. BAXTER.

Oh, really, Miss Roberts, I can't be pinned down like that. [*She moves towards* MR. BAXTER.] Aren't you and Miss Roberts going to play chess?

MR. BAXTER.

[*Rising.*] Miss Roberts seems so anxious to have this thing decided. I told her that anything to do with the girls' education was left to *you*.

MRS. BAXTER.

Need it be settled this minute?

Miss ROBERTS.

[*Going towards* MRS. BAXTER.] I've tried so often to speak to you about it and something must be done.

MRS. BAXTER.

[*Resigning herself.*] Of course—if you insist upon it—I'll do it now. I'll do anything any of you wish. [*She sits down.*] I've had a slight headache all day—it's rather worse since dinner; I really ought to be in bed, but I wanted to be up when Tom comes. If I begin to discuss this now I shall be in no state to receive him—but, of course—if you insist—

Miss ROBERTS.

I don't want to tire you.

MRS. BAXTER.

It *would* tire me very much.

Miss ROBERTS.

Then I suppose we must put it off again.

Act I

MRS. BAXTER.

[*Smiling.*] I think that would be best. We must thrash it out properly—some day.

[*She leans back in her chair.*]

MR. BAXTER.

[*To* Miss ROBERTS, *sighing.*] I suppose we may as well play chess?

Miss ROBERTS.

[*With resignation.*] I suppose so.

[MR. BAXTER *and* Miss ROBERTS *sit at a table and arrange the chess men.*]

MRS. BAXTER.

[*Finding her place in her magazine, begins to read. After a slight pause, she says.*] What an abominable light! I can't possibly see to read. I suppose, Miss Roberts, you couldn't possibly carry that lamp over to this table, could you? [Miss ROBERTS *makes a alight movement as though she would fetch the lamp.*] It's too heavy, isn't it?

MR. BAXTER.

Much too heavy!

MRS. BAXTER.

I thought so. I'm afraid I must strain my eyes. I can't bear to sit idle.

MR. BAXTER.

[*Rising.*] I'll carry the lamp over.

MRS. BAXTER.

[*Quickly.*] No, no! You'd spill it. Call one of the servants; wouldn't that be the simplest plan?

MR. BAXTER.

The simplest plan would be for you to walk over to the lamp.

MRS. BAXTER.

Certainly, dear, if it's too much trouble to call one of the servants. [*She rises and carries her magazine to a chair by the lamp.*] I wouldn't have said anything about the lamp if I'd thought it was going to be such a business to move it. [*She sits and turns over a page or two while* MR. BAXTER, *who has returned to his seat, and* Miss ROBERTS *continue arranging the chess board.* MRS. BAXTER *calls gaily over her shoulder.*] Have you checkmated Mr. Baxter yet, Miss Roberts?

Miss ROBERTS.

I haven't finished setting the board.

MRS. BAXTER.

How slow you are. [*She turns a page or two idly, then says seriously to* MR. BAXTER.] Dear, you'll be interested to know that I don't think the housemaid opposite is engaged to young Locker. I believe it's the cook.

MR. BAXTER.

Very interesting, dear. [*To* Miss ROBERTS.] It's you to play.

[*After three moves of chess,* MRS. BAXTER *says.*]

ACT I

MRS. BAXTER.

Oh, here's such a clever article on wasps. It seems that wasps—I'll read you what it says. [*She clears her throat.*] Wasps—

MR. BAXTER.

[*Plaintively.*] Dulcie, dear, it's impossible for us to give our minds to the game if you read aloud.

MRS. BAXTER.

[*Amiably.*] I'm so sorry, dear. I didn't mean to disturb you. I think you'd have found the article instructive. If you want to read it afterwards, it's page 32, if you can remember that. "Wasps and all about them." I'll dog-ear the page. Oh, I never looked out Tom's train. Miss Roberts, you'll find the time-table on the hall table. [Miss ROBERTS *rises and* MRS. BAXTER *goes on.*] Or if it isn't there, it may be—

Miss ROBERTS.

[*Quickly.*] I know where it is.

[*She goes out.*]

MRS. BAXTER.

What has Miss Roberts been saying to you about leaving?

MR. BAXTER.

Only what she said to you.

MRS. BAXTER.

I hope she won't leave me before I get suited. I shall never find any one else to suit me. I don't know what I should do without Miss Roberts.

Act I

[Miss ROSEN ROBERTS *re-enters with small time-table.*]

Miss ROBERTS.
Here it is!

MRS. BAXTER.
[*Cheerfully.*] Thank you, Miss Roberts, but I've just remembered he isn't coming by train at all; he's coming in a motor car.

MR. BAXTER.
All the way from London?

MRS. BAXTER.
Yes, at least I think so. It's all in his letter. Who knows what I did with Tom's letter?

Miss ROBERTS.
[*Making a slight movement as if to go.*] Shall I go and look?

MRS. BAXTER.
Hush. I'm trying to think where I put it. [*Staring in front of her.*] I had it in my hand before tea. I remember dropping it—I had it again after tea; I remember thinking it was another letter, but it wasn't. That's how I know. [*Then to the others.*] I'm surprised neither of you remembers where I put it.

Miss ROBERTS.
I'd better go and look.

[*She moves to go.*]

MR. BAXTER.

I think I hear a motor coming.

[*He goes and looks through the window.*]

MRS. BAXTER.

[*In an injured tone.*] It's too late now, Miss Roberts. Mr. Baxter thinks he hears a motor coming.

MR. BAXTER.

Yes, it is a car; I see the lamps. It must be Tom.

MRS. BAXTER.

[*Smiling affectionately.*] Dear Tom, how nice it will be to see him again. [*To* MR. BAXTER.] Aren't you going to the hall to meet Tom?

MR. BAXTER.

Yes, of course.

[*He goes out.*]

MRS. BAXTER.

You've never seen my brother Tom.

Miss ROBERTS.

No, I don't think he's been home since I came to you.

MRS. BAXTER.

No, I was trying to count up this afternoon how many years it would be since Tom was home. I've forgotten again now, but I know I did it; you'd be surprised.

Act I

TOM.

[*Outside.*] Where is she?

[*Confused greetings between* TOM *and* MR. BAXTER *are heard.* MRS. BAXTER *rises smiling, and goes towards the stairs.*]

MRS. BAXTER.

That's Tom's voice.

[TOM KEMP *enters followed by* MR. BAXTER. TOM *is a cheerful, genial, high-spirited man about forty-five; he comes down-stairs, where* MRS. BAXTER *meets him. He takes her in both arms and kisses her on each cheek.*]

TOM.

Well, child, how are you—bless you.

MRS. BAXTER.

Oh, Tom, it is nice to see you again.

TOM.

[*Holding her off and looking at her.*] You look just the same.

MRS. BAXTER.

So do you, Tom. I'm so glad you haven't grown fat.

TOM.

[*Laughing.*] No chance to grow fat out there. Life is too strenuous. [*He turns to* MR. BAXTER *and gives him a slap on his back.*] Well, Dick, you old duffer.

MRS. BAXTER.

Tom.

TOM.

[*Turning to her.*] Yes?

MRS. BAXTER.

I want to introduce you to Miss Roberts. [TOM *gives* Miss ROBERTS *a friendly hand-shake.*]

TOM.

How d'you do, Miss Roberts?

MRS. BAXTER.

Are you very tired, Tom?

TOM.

Tired—no—never tired. [*Smiling at* MRS. BAXTER.] You look splendid. [*He holds her by her shoulders.*]

MRS. BAXTER.

[*Languidly.*] I'm pretty well.

TOM.

[*Spinning* MRS. BAXTER *round.*] Never better.

MRS. BAXTER.

[*Disliking such treatment.*] I'm pretty well. [*She wriggles her shoulders and edges away.*]

MR. BAXTER.

[*To* TOM.] Have you dined?

TOM.

Magnificently. Soup—fish—chops—roast beef—[*To* Miss ROBERTS.] You must live in Colorado, Miss Roberts, if you want to relish roast beef.

MR. BAXTER.

But you've driven from London since dinner. [*To* MRS. BAXTER.] I suppose we can raise him a supper?

MRS. BAXTER.

If the things aren't all put away.

TOM.

[*Turning from* Miss ROBERTS.] No—see here—hold on—I dined at the Inn.

MRS. BAXTER.

[*Smiling graciously.*] Oh, I was just going to offer to go into the kitchen and cook you something myself.

[*She sits.*]

TOM.

I was late getting in and I wasn't sure what time you dined. [*To* MR. BAXTER.] Now, Dick, tell me the family history.

MR. BAXTER.

[*Scratching his head, says slowly.*] The family history?

MRS. BAXTER.

[*Calling out suddenly.*] His! Ablative—his.

TOM.

Eh?

MRS. BAXTER.

[*Gravely to TOM.*] Hic—haec—hoc. His—his—his.

ACT I

TOM.

[*Looking blankly a*t Miss ROBERTS *and* MR. BAXTER.] What's the matter?

MRS. BAXTER.

[*Smiling as she explains.*] I was giving them a Latin lesson before you came.

TOM.

[*Amused.*] You?

MRS. BAXTER.

[*Conceitedly.*] I never think we were meant to spend all our time in frivolous conversation.

TOM.

[*Amused, turning to* MR. BAXTER.] Dulcie, giving you a Latin lesson?

MR. BAXTER.

[*Sadly.*] I suppose she really thinks she was by now.

TOM.

[*Walking about.*] It's bully to be home again. I felt like a kid coming here—slipping along in the dark—with English trees and English hedges and English farms flitting by. No one awake but a few English cows, standing in the fields—up to their knees in mist. It looked like dreams—like that dream I sometimes have out there in Colorado. I dream I've just arrived in England—with no baggage and nothing on but my pyjamas.

MRS. BAXTER.
What *is* he talking about?

Miss ROBERTS.
I know what you mean!

TOM.
I guess you've had that dream yourself. No, I mean you know how I must have felt.

Miss ROBERTS.
Like a ghost revisiting its old haunts.

TOM.
[*Sitting near* Miss ROBERTS.] Like the ghost of the boy I used to be. I thought you'd understand. You look as if you would.

MRS. BAXTER.
I'm so glad you haven't married some nasty common person in America.

TOM.
[*Chaffingly to he*r.] I thought you would be. That's why I didn't do it.

[*He talks to* Miss ROBERTS.]

MRS. BAXTER.
[*Laughing as she turns to say to* MR. BAXTER.] He's always so full of fun.

ACT I

MISS ROBERTS.

I once dreamed I was in Colorado—but it was only from one of those picture post-cards you sent. I have never travelled.

TOM.

And how did Colorado look in your dreams?

MISS ROBERTS.

[*Recalling her vision of Colorado.*] Forests—

TOM.

That's right. Pine forests stretching away, away—down below there in the valley—a sea of tree-tops waving—waving—waving for miles.

MISS ROBERTS.

And mountains.

TOM.

Chains of mountains—great blue mountains streaked with snow—range beyond range. Oh! it's grand! it's great!

MISS ROBERTS.

I should love to see it.

MRS. BAXTER.

I think you are much better off where you are, Miss Roberts.

TOM.

It's great, but it's not gentle like this. It doesn't make you want to cry. It only makes you want to say your prayers.

Act I

MRS. BAXTER.

[*Laughing as she turns to* MR. BAXTER.] Isn't he droll?

MISS ROBERTS.

I know what you mean.

TOM.

You know. I thought *you'd* know. Here it comes so close to you; it's so cozy and personal. They've nothing like our orchards and lawns out there. [*Rising suddenly.*] I want to smell the garden. [*He goes to the window.*]

MR. BAXTER.

No! Tom, Tom!

MRS. BAXTER

Don't open the window; we shall all catch cold.

TOM.

[*Laughing as he comes towards* MRS. BAXTER.] Dear old Dulcie, same as ever.

MRS. BAXTER.

[*Smiling.*] All of us are not accustomed to living in tents and huts and such places.

TOM.

What are you going to do with me in the morning?

MRS. BAXTER.

We might all take a little walk, if it's a nice day.

TOM.
A little walk!

MRS. BAXTER.
If we're not too tired after the excitement of your arrival.

TOM.
What time's breakfast?

MR. BAXTER.
Quarter to nine.

MRS. BAXTER.
We drift down about half-past.

TOM.
What! You've got an English garden, and it's summer time and you aren't all running about outside at six o'clock in the morning?

Miss ROBERTS.
I am.

TOM.
You are? Yes, I thought you would be. *You* and I must have a walk before breakfast tomorrow morning.

Miss ROBERTS.
[*Smiling.*] Very well.

MRS. BAXTER.
Don't overdo yourself, Miss Roberts, before you begin the duties of the day. [*To* TOM.] Miss Roberts is the children's governess.

ACT I

TOM.

Oh? [*To* Miss ROBERTS.] Do you rap them over the knuckles? And stick them in the corner?

Miss ROBERTS.

[*Answering him in the same spirit of raillery.*] Oh, yes—pinch them and slap them and box their ears.

MRS. BAXTER.

[*Leaning forward in her chair, thinking this may be true.*] I hope you don't do anything of the sort, Miss Roberts.

Miss ROBERTS.

Oh, no! not really, Mrs. Baxter. [*She rises.*] I think I'll say good-night.

TOM.

Don't go to bed yet, Miss Roberts.

MRS. BAXTER.

[*Yawning.*] It's about time we all went.

TOM.

[*To* MRS. BAXTER.] You, too?

MRS. BAXTER.

What time is it?

TOM.

[*Looking at his watch.*] Twenty minutes past ten.

MRS. BAXTER.

How late.

ACT I

TOM.
Call that late?

MRS. BAXTER.

Ten is our bedtime. [*She rises.*] Come along, Miss Roberts; we shan't be fit for anything in the morning if we don't bustle off to bed. [*She suppresses a yawn.*]

MISS ROBERTS.
Good-night, Mr. Baxter.

[*She shakes hands with him.*]

MR. BAXTER.
Good-night.

MISS ROBERTS.
[*Shaking hands with* TOM.] Good-night.

TOM.
Good-night, Miss Roberts; sleep well.

MISS ROBERTS.
I always do.

MRS. BAXTER.

Will you give me the magazine off the table, Miss Roberts, to take up-stairs? [TOM *goes to the table and hands the magazine to* Miss ROBERTS, *who brings it to* MRS. BAXTER. *To* Miss ROBERTS.] You and I needn't say good-night. We shall meet on the landing.

[*Turns over the pages of the magazine.*]

ACT I

MISS ROBERTS.

Good-night, everybody.

TOM.

[*Following* Miss ROBERTS *to the foot of the stair*s.] Good-night, Miss Roberts. [Miss ROBERTS goes out.] Nice girl, Miss Roberts.

MRS. BAXTER.

She suits me very well.

MR. BAXTER.

She says she is going to leave.

TOM.

Leave—Miss Roberts mustn't leave!

MRS. BAXTER.

I don't think she meant it. Don't sit up too late, Tom, and don't hurry down in the morning. Would you like your breakfast in bed?

TOM.

[*Laughing.*] In bed?

MRS. BAXTER.

I thought you'd be so worn out after your journey.

TOM.

Heavens, no, that's nothing. Good-night, little sister. [*He kisses her.*]

Act I

MRS. BAXTER.

Good-night, Tom. It's so nice to see you again. [*Then to* MR. BAXTER.] Try not to disturb me when you come up-stairs. [*Speaking through a yawn as she goes towards the door.*] Oh, dear, I'm so sleepy. [*She goes out.*]

MR. BAXTER.

[*Smiling at* TOM.] Well, Tom!

TOM.

[*Smiling at* MR. BAXTER.] Well, Dick, how's everything? Business pretty good?

MR. BAXTER.

So so.

TOM.

That's nice.

MR. BAXTER.

I don't go into the city every day now—two or three times a week. I leave my partners to attend to things the rest of the time—they seem to get on just as well without me.

TOM.

I dare say they would. [*Taking out his cigarette case.*] I suppose I may smoke?

MR. BAXTER.

[*Doubtfully.*] Here?

TOM.

Well, don't you smoke here?

MR. BAXTER.

You may. She won't smell it in the morning. [TOM *laughs and takes out a cigarette.*] Tom, if ever you get married don't give in to your wife's weaknesses in the first few days of the honeymoon—you'll want to then, but don't. It becomes a habit. What's the use of saying that to you? I suppose you'll never marry now. [*He sits down.*]

TOM.

[*Quite annoyed.*] Why not? Why shouldn't I marry? I don't see why you think I shan't marry. How long has she been here?

[*He lights a cigarette.*]

MR. BAXTER.
Who?

TOM.
Miss Roberts.

MR. BAXTER.
Oh!

TOM.
Weren't we talking of Miss Roberts?

MR. BAXTER.
No.

TOM.
Oh, well, we are now.

ACT I

MR. BAXTER.

She's been here about four years. I'm so sorry she wants to leave. I don't want her to go at all.

TOM.

Nor do I. Rather nice for you, Dick. A pretty wife and a pretty governess.

[*He nudges him.*]

MR. BAXTER.

Tom, don't do that.

[*He defends himself by putting up his hands.*]

TOM.

Very well, I won't.

MR. BAXTER.

[*Embarrassed and slightly annoyed.*] Why do you say that?

TOM.

Only chaffing. [*He sees the chess-board.*] Who's been playing chess?

MR. BAXTER.

Miss Roberts and I.

TOM.

Does Miss Roberts play chess? I must get her to teach me—let me see if I can remember any of the moves. [*He sits by the table and moves the chess men about idly as he talks.*] She is far too good to be your governess.

Act I

MR. BAXTER.

[*Enthusing.*] You've noticed what an unusual woman she is?

TOM.

Charming!

MR. BAXTER.

Isn't she?

TOM.

And so pretty!

MR BAXTER.

Very pretty.

TOM.

She'll make a good wife for some man.

MR. BAXTER.

[*Reluctantly.*] I suppose so—sometime.

TOM.

I should make love to her if I lived in the same house.

MR. BAXTER.

But if you were married?

TOM.

I'm not!

MR. BAXTER.

[*Slowly and thoughtfully.*] No.

[*There is a moment's pause.*]

TOM.

Let's change the subject, and talk about Miss Roberts. Tell me things about her.

MR. BAXTER.

She's an orphan.

TOM.

Poor girl.

MR. BAXTER.

She's no near relations.

TOM.

Lucky fellow.

MR. BAXTER.

She's wonderful with the children.

TOM.

Make a good mother.

MR. BAXTER.

And so nice, so interesting, so good, such a companion. I can't find a single fault in her. She's a woman in a thousand, in a million.

TOM.

I say, you'd better not let Dulcie hear you talk like that.

MR. BAXTER.

[*Seriously.*] I don't. [TOM *laughs.*] I was only saying that to show you how well she suits us.

ACT I

TOM.
Of course.

MR. BAXTER.
How well she suits Dulcie.

TOM.
Oh, Dulcie, of course.

MR. BAXTER.
I can't think what Dulcie will do without her; she's got so used to her. Miss Roberts waits on Dulcie hand and foot.

TOM.
[*Indignantly*]. What a shame!

MR. BAXTER.
Isn't it?

TOM.
Why should Dulcie be waited on hand and foot?

MR. BAXTER.
I don't know. She's so—well, not exactly ill.

TOM.
Ill? She's as strong as a horse, always was.

MR. BAXTER.
Yes, I can't remember when she had anything really the matter with her, but she always seems so tired—keeps wanting to lie down—she's not an invalid, she's a—

ACT I

TOM.
She's a mollusc.

MR. BAXTER.
What's that?

TOM.
Mollusca, subdivision of the animal kingdom.

MR. BAXTER.
I know that.

TOM.
I don't know if the Germans have remarked that many mammalia display characteristics commonly assigned to mollusca. I suppose the scientific explanation is that a mollusc once married a mammal and their descendants are the human mollusc.

MR. BAXTER.
[*Much puzzled.*] What are you talking about?

TOM.
People who are like a mollusc of the sea, which clings to a rock and lets the tide flow over its head. People who spend all their energy and ingenuity in sticking instead of moving, in whom the instinct for what I call molluscry is as dominating as an inborn vice. And it is so catching. Why, one mollusc will infect a whole household. We all had it at home. Mother was quite a famous mollusc in her time.

She was bedridden for fifteen years, and then, don't you remember, got up to Dulcie's wedding, to the amazement of everybody, and tripped down the aisle as lively as a kitten, and then went to bed again till she heard of something else she wanted to go to—a garden party or something. Father, he was a mollusc, too; he called it being a conservative; he might just as well have stayed in bed, too. Ada, Charlie, Emmeline, all of them were more or less mollusky, but Dulcibella was the queen. You won't often see such a fine healthy specimen of a mollusc as Dulcie. I'm a born mollusc!

MR. BAXTER.

[*Surprised.*] You?

TOM.

Yes, I'm energetic now, but only artificially energetic. I have to be on to myself all the time; make myself do things. That's why I chose the vigorous West, and wander from camp to camp. I made a pile in Leadville. I gambled it all away. I made another in Cripple Creek. I gave it away to the poor. If I made another, I should chuck it away. Don't you see why? Give me a competence, nothing to work for, nothing to worry about from day to day—why I should become as famous a mollusc as dear old mother was.

MR. BAXTER.

Is molluscry the same as laziness?

TOM.

No, not altogether. The lazy flow with the tide. The mollusc uses forces to resist pressure. It's amazing the amount of force a mollusc will use, to do nothing, when it would be so much easier to do something. It's no fool, you know, it's often the most artful creature, it wriggles and squirms, and even fights from the instinct not to advance. There are wonderful things about molluscry, things to make you shout with laughter, but it's sad enough, too—it can ruin a life so, not only the life of the mollusc, but all the lives in the house where it dwells.

MR. BAXTER.

Is there no cure for molluscry?

TOM.

Well, I should say once a mollusc always a mollusc. But it's like drink, or any other vice. If grappled with it can be kept under. If left to itself, it becomes incurable.

MR. BAXTER.

Is Dulcie a very advanced case?

TOM.

Oh, very!!!

MR. BAXTER.

Oh!

TOM.

But let us hope not incurable. You know better than I how far she has gone. Tell me.

MR. BAXTER.

[*Seriously.*] She's certainly getting worse. For instance, I can remember the time when she would go to church twice a Sunday, walk there and back; now she drives once, and she keeps an extra cushion in the pew, sits down for the hymns and makes the girls find her places.

TOM.

Do you ever tell her not to mollusc so much?

MR. BAXTER.

I used to, but I've given up now.

TOM.

Oh, you must never give up.

MR. BAXTER.

The trouble is she thinks she's so very active.

TOM.

Molluscs always think that.

MR. BAXTER.

Dulcie thinks of something to be done and tells me to do it, and then, by some mental process, which I don't pretend to grasp, she thinks she's done it herself. D'you think she does that to humbug me?

TOM.

I believe there's no dividing line between the conscious and subconscious thoughts of molluscs. She probably humbugs herself just as much as she humbugs you.

MR. BAXTER.

Oh!

TOM.

You must be firm with her. The next time she tells you to do a thing, tell her to do it herself.

MR. BAXTER.

I tried that. The other day, for instance, she wanted me to set a mouse-trap in her dressing-room; well, I was very busy at the time, and I knew there were no mice there, so I refused. It meant getting the cheese and everything.

TOM.

[*Trying not to appear amused.*] Of course. And what did she say when you refused to set the mouse-trap?

MR. BAXTER.

She began to make me sorry for her; she has no end of ways of making me sorry for her, and I've a very tender heart; but that day I just didn't care. I had the devil in me, so I said—set it yourself.

TOM.

Bravo.

MR. BAXTER.

We got quite unpleasant over it.

TOM.

And which of you set the mouse-trap in the end?

MR. BAXTER.

Miss Roberts. [TOM *rises and moves away to hide his amusement from* MR. BAXTER.] It's always like that. She makes Miss Roberts do everything. For instance, Dulcie used to play chess with me of an evening, now she tells Miss Roberts to. She used to go walks with me, now she sends Miss Roberts. Dulcie was never energetic, but we used to have some good times together; now I can't get her to go anywhere or do anything.

TOM.
Not very amusing for *you*.

MR. BAXTER.
It does rather take the fun out of everything.

TOM.
How did you come to let her get so bad?

MR. BAXTER.
[*Simply.*] I fell in love with her. That put me at her mercy.

[*There is a moment's silence, then* TOM *says with decision.*]

TOM.
I must take her in hand.

MR. BAXTER.
I wish you would.

TOM.
I'll make her dance.

MR. BAXTER.
Don't be hard on her.

TOM.
No, but firm. I'll show her what firmness is. A brother is the best person in the world to undertake the education of a mollusc. His firmness will be tempered with affection, and his affection won't be undermined with sentimentality. I shall start in on Dulcie the first thing tomorrow morning.

ACT I ✿

MR. BAXTER.

And now what do you say to getting our candles?

TOM.

[*Following* MR. BAXTER *towards the stairs.*] Come along. I'm ready—must have a good night's rest if I'm to tackle Dulcie in the morning. I don't anticipate any trouble. A woman isn't difficult to deal with if you take her the right way. Leave her to me, old man. You just leave her to me!

[*They go up the stairs as the curtain falls.*]

The Second Act

SCENE. *The same scene on the following morning. The French windows are wide open, displaying a view of the garden bathed in sunshine.*

MRS. BAXTER *is lounging in an armchair reading a novel.* TOM *enters with an enormous bunch of wild flowers, foxgloves, meadow-sweet, etc.*

Act II

TOM.

Look!

MRS. BAXTER.

Oh, how pretty! We must put them in water. Where's Miss Roberts?

TOM.

In the schoolroom. They are at their lessons.

MRS. BAXTER.

Then we must wait. What a pity. I hope they won't die.

TOM.

Is Miss Roberts the only person in this house who can put these flowers in water?

MRS. BAXTER.

The servants are always busy in the morning.

TOM.

Why can't *you* do it?

MRS. BAXTER.

I have other things to do.

TOM.

What?

MRS. BAXTER.

Numerous things. Do you think a woman never has anything to do?

ACT II ✸

TOM.

[*Coming to her and tapping her on the shoulder.*] Get up and do them yourself.

MRS. BAXTER.

[*Amiably.*] While you sit still in this chair. All very fine!

TOM.

I'll help you.

MRS. BAXTER.

[*Rising lazily.*] Very well. Bring me the vases and some water. [*She smells the flowers.*]

TOM.

Vases. [*Pointing to two vases on the mantel-piece.*] Will these do?

MRS. BAXTER.

Yes. Get those.

TOM.

[*Pointing to another vase on the table.*] And that. You must get that one. We will divide the labour. [*He gets the two vases.* MRS. BAXTER *has not stirred.*] Where's yours?

MRS. BAXTER.

[*Smiling pleasantly.*] I thought *you* were going to get the vases.

TOM.

We were going to do this work between us. Get your vase.

Act II

MRS. BAXTER.

[*Laughing.*] Oh, Tom—what a boy you are still.

TOM.

Why should I get all the vases? [*Talking seriously to her.*] You know, Dulcie, you'd feel better if you ran about a little more.

MRS. BAXTER.

[*Pleasantly.*] You'd save time, dear, if you'd run and get that vase yourself instead of standing there telling me to.

[TOM *puts the vases on the table. Then he goes and takes up the other vase.*]

TOM.

Oh, very well. It's not worth quarreling about.

MRS. BAXTER.

No, don't let us quarrel the first morning you are home.

TOM.

[*Bringing the vase and putting it before her.*] There!

MRS. BAXTER.

Thank you, Tom. You'll find a tap in the wall outside the window and a little watering-can beside it.

TOM.

I got the vases.

MRS. BAXTER.

Please bring me the water, Tom. These poppies are beginning to droop already.

Act II ✺

TOM.

I *won't* get the water. You must get it yourself.

MRS. BAXTER.

[*Smiling.*] Very well. Wait till I go upstairs and put on my hat.

TOM.

To go just outside the window?

MRS. BAXTER.

I can't go into the hot sun without a hat.

TOM.

Rats!

MRS. BAXTER.

[*Seriously.*] It's *not* rats. Dr. Ross said I must *never* go out in the sun without a hat.

TOM.

That much won't hurt you.

MRS. BAXTER.

I don't mind, of course. But *you* must take the consequences if I have a sunstroke. Dick will be furious when he hears I've been out in the sun without a hat. You wouldn't like me to make Dick furious, would you, Tom? [TOM *touches her and points to the window, then folds his arms. There is a slight pause while she waits for* TOM *to offer to go.*] If you think it's too much trouble to step outside the window I'll go all the way upstairs for my hat. I suppose all these pretty flowers will be quite dead by the time I come back.

Act II

TOM.

[*Exasperated.*] Oh, very well, I'll get the water.

[*He goes out into the garden.*]

MRS. BAXTER.

[*Calling.*] Try not to scratch the can, and be sure you don't leave the tap to dribble.

TOM.

[*Outside.*] Oh, the tap's all right.

[*She occupies herself by smelling the flowers.* TOM *re-enters almost immediately with a little watering-can.*]

TOM.

Here's the water.

MRS. BAXTER.

Thank you, Tom. Work seems like play when we do it between us. Fill the vases.

TOM.

I won't. [*He puts the can on the table.*]

MRS. BAXTER.

Well, wait while I go and get an apron.

TOM.

You don't want an apron for that.

Act II

MRS. BAXTER.

I'm not going to risk spilling the water all down this dress; I only put it on so as to look nice for you. I won't be a minute.

TOM.

Stay where you are. [*Muttering to himself as he fills the vases.*] An apron to fill three vases. You might as well put on your boots, or get an umbrella or a waterproof. [*He is about to set the can on the floor.*]

MRS. BAXTER.

[*Quickly.*] Don't put it on the carpet. Put it on the gravel outside.

TOM.

Put it on the gravel yourself.

[TOM *holds the can for her to take. She elaborately begins to wind a handkerchief round her right hand.*]

MRS. BAXTER.

It's no use both of us wetting our hands.

[TOM *grumbing goes to the window and pitches the can outside.*]

TOM.

Now I hope I've scratched the can, and I'm sorry I didn't leave the tap to dribble.

MRS. BAXTER.

Naughty, naughty. Do you remember, Tom, when we were all at home together, you always did the flowers?

Act II

TOM.

I'm not going to do them now.

MRS. BAXTER.

You did them so tastefully. No one could do flowers like you. I remember Aunt Lizzie calling one day and saying if we hired a florist to arrange our flowers, we couldn't have got prettier effects than you got.

TOM.

Get on with those flowers.

MRS. BAXTER.

When I did the flowers, Mamma used to say the drawing-room used to look like a rubbish heap.

TOM.

[*Loudly.*] Get on with those flowers.

MRS. BAXTER.

I should so like Miss Roberts to see the way you can arrange flowers.

TOM.

Get on—

MRS. BAXTER.

[*Wheedling him.*] Do arrange one vase—only one, just to show Miss Roberts.

TOM.

[*Weakening.*] Well, only one. You must do the other two.

Act II

[*He begins to put the flowers in water.* MRS. BAXTER *watches him a moment, then she sinks into the handiest arm-chair.*]

MRS. BAXTER.

[*After a slight pause.*] How well you do it.

TOM.

[*Suddenly realizing the situation.*] No, no, I won't. [*He flings the flowers on the table.*] Oh, you are artful. You've done nothing; I've done everything; I got the flowers, the vases, the water—everything, and now not another stalk will I touch. I don't care if they die; their blood will be on your head, not mine.

[*He sits down and folds his arms. A pause.*]

MRS. BAXTER.

[*Serenely.*] If you won't talk, I may as well go on reading my novel. It's on the table beside you. Would you mind passing it?

TOM.

Yes, I would.

MRS. BAXTER.

Throw it.

TOM.

I shan't.

MRS. BAXTER.

I thought you'd cheer us up when you came home, but you just sit in my chair doing nothing.

Act II

TOM.

[*Turning to her and saying gravely.*] Dulcie, it grieves me very much to see you such a Mollusc.

MRS. BAXTER.

What's a Mollusc?

TOM.

You are.

MRS. BAXTER.

[*Puzzled.*] A Mollusc? [*Gaily.*] Oh, I know, one of those pretty little creatures that live in the sea—or am I thinking of a sea anemone?

TOM.

It's dreadful to see a strong healthy woman so idle.

MRS. BAXTER.

[*Genuinely amazed.*] I idle? Oh, you're joking.

TOM.

What are you doing but idling now? [*Approaching her and saying roughly.*] Get up, and do those flowers. Get out of that chair this minute.

MRS. BAXTER.

[*Rising and smiling.*] I was only waiting for you. I thought we were going to do the flowers together.

TOM.

No, we won't do them together; if we do them together I shall be doing them by myself before I know where I am. [*He sits again.*]

Act II ✻

MRS. BAXTER.

I don't call that fair, to promise to help me with the flowers, and then just to sit and watch. I don't think Colorado is improving you. You've become so lazy and underhand.

TOM.

[*Indignantly.*] What do you mean?

MRS. BAXTER.

What I mean to say is, you undertook to help me with the flowers, and now you try to back out of it. Perhaps you call that sharp in America, but in England we should call it un-sportsmanlike.

TOM.

[*Picking up the flowers and throwing them down disgustedly.*] Oh, why did I ever go and gather all this rubbish?

[MR. BAXTER *enters and comes down the stairs.*]

MR. BAXTER.

Half-past eleven, dear.

MRS. BAXTER.

Thank you, dear.

TOM.

Half-past eleven, dear—thank you, dear—what does that mean?

MR. BAXTER.

Lunch.

ACT II

TOM.

Already?

MR. BAXTER.

Not real lunch.

MRS. BAXTER.

We always have cake and milk in the dining-room at half-past eleven. We think it breaks up the morning more. Aren't you coming?

TOM.

Cake and milk at half-past eleven; what an idea! No, thank you.

MRS. BAXTER.

I shall be glad of the chance to sit down. I've had a most exhausting morning.

[*She goes out.*]

MR. BAXTER.

Have you been taking her in hand?

TOM.

[*Pretending not to comprehend.*] I beg your pardon?

MR. BAXTER.

You said you were going to take her in hand, first thing this morning.

TOM.

Oh, yes, so I did. So I have done—in a way—not seriously, of course not the first morning.

Act II

MR. BAXTER.

You said you were going to show her what firmness was.

TOM.

Well, so I did, but never having had any firmness from you, she doesn't know it when she sees it. [*MR. BAXTER is about to put some of the flowers in a vase.*] What are you doing?

MR. BAXTER.

They're dying for want of water.

TOM.

But I said she must put them in water herself.

MR. BAXTER.

Oh, I see, discipline.

TOM.

Exactly.

MR. BAXTER.

What happened?

TOM.

[*Pointing to the flowers.*] Can't you see what's happened? There they are still. [*Angrily.*] We've spent hours wrangling over those damned flowers. It may seem paltry to make such a fuss over anything so trivial, but it's the principle of the thing; if I give in at the start, I shall have to give in to the finish.

Act II

MR. BAXTER.

Like me.

TOM.

Yes, like you. When she comes back from the dining-room, I'll make her do those flowers herself, if I have to stand over her all the morning.

MR. BAXTER.

[*Looking at* TOM *with admiration.*] That's the spirit. If only I had begun like that the very first morning of our honeymoon.

TOM.

[*With great determination.*] I'll stand no nonsense. She shall do the flowers herself.

[Miss ROBERTS *enters.*]

Miss ROBERTS.

Mrs. Baxter sent me to do the flowers.

[*She comes immediately to the table and begins putting the flowers in water.* TOM *and* MR. BAXTER *look at each other.*]

TOM.

[*To him.*] Shall I tell her not to?

MR. BAXTER.

Then Dulcie will tell her she is to.

Act II

TOM.

Then we shall have to humiliate Dulcie before Miss Roberts.

MR. BAXTER.

Yes.

TOM.

I don't want to do that.

MR. BAXTER.

No.

TOM.

I'm not giving in.

MR. BAXTER.

No.

TOM.

Don't gloat.

MR. BAXTER.

I'm not gloating.

TOM.

You are. You're gloating because I've had to give in the way *you* always do.

MISS ROBERTS.

[*To* MR. BAXTER.] The girls have been asking if I thought they could have a half-holiday in honour of their uncle's arrival.

Act II

MR. BAXTER.

I don't see why not.

Miss ROBERTS.

If you think they'd be in the way, I might take them off to the woods for the day.

MR. BAXTER.

Yes.

Miss ROBERTS.

I thought as it's so fine we might take our lunch with us, and have a picnic.

TOM.

Why don't we all go a picnic?

MR. BAXTER.

All who?

TOM.

You and I and the girls and Miss Roberts and Dulcie.

MR. BAXTER.

You'll never get Dulcie on a picnic, will he, Miss Roberts?

TOM.

Why not?

MR. BAXTER.

Too much exertion.

Act II ✿

Miss ROBERTS.

[*Still busy filling the vases.*] I think Mrs. Baxter would go if Mr. Kemp asked her.

[TOM *looks at* MR. BAXTER *as soon as* Miss ROBERTS *has spoken and* MR. BAXTER *looks dubious.*]

TOM.

[*In a lower voice, to* MR. BAXTER.] I don't want Miss Roberts to think that I can't master Dulcie; besides, a picnic, the very thing to make her run about, but we must approach her tactfully and keep our tempers. I lost mine over the flowers, otherwise I've not the least doubt I could have made her do them; we must humour Dulcie and cajole her. Whisk her off to the woods in a whirl of gaiety; you go dancing into the dining-room like this. [*Assuming great jollity.*] We're all going off on a picnic.

MR. BAXTER.
Oh, no.

TOM.
Why not?

MR. BAXTER.
It wouldn't be me.

TOM.

Well, er—[glancing at Miss ROBERTS] go and—er—[*Glancing again at* Miss ROBERTS.] Oh, go and say whatever you like. But be jolly about it; full of the devil.

[*He takes* MR. BAXTER *by the arm and pushes him towards the stairs.*]

Act II

MR. BAXTER.

[*Imitating* TOM *as he goes.*] We're all going off on a picnic. [*He stops at the top of the stairs and says seriously.*] It wouldn't be me.

[*He exits.*]

TOM.

So you're not one of the cake and milk brigade?

Miss ROBERTS.

No.

TOM.

I thought you wouldn't be.

Miss ROBERTS.

Aren't you going to join them?

TOM.

No, I don't want to eat cake in the middle of the morning. I'm like you. We seem to have a lot of habits in common.

Miss ROBERTS.

Do you think so?

TOM.

Don't you?

Miss ROBERTS.

I haven't thought.

Act II ❊

[*She takes a vase to the mantelpiece.* TOM *watches her and follows with the other vase.* Miss ROBERTS. *takes the vase from* TOM *and puts it on the mantelpiece.*]

TOM.

Didn't we have a nice walk together?

Miss ROBERTS.

Yes; don't you love being out in the early morning?

TOM.

I'm up with the sun at home out West. I live out-of-doors out there.

Miss ROBERTS.

How splendid!

TOM.

You're the kind of girl for Colorado.

Miss ROBERTS.

[*Pleased.*] Am I?

TOM.

Can you ride?

Miss ROBERTS.

Yes, but I don't get any opportunities now.

TOM.

Got a good nerve?

Act II

Miss ROBERTS.

I broke a colt once; he'd thrown three men, but he never threw me!

TOM.

[*Smiling at her.*] Well done!

Miss ROBERTS.

I didn't mean to boast, but I'd love to do it again.

TOM.

I should love to see you mounted on a mustang, flying through our country.

Miss ROBERTS.

With the tree tops waving down in the valley, and the great blue mountains you told us about, stretching away—away—

TOM.

[*Watching her with admiration.*] You certainly ought to come to Colorado.

Miss ROBERTS.

Nothing so thrilling could happen to me.

[*She returns to the table and picks up the remaining flowers.*]

TOM.

[*following her.*] Why? You've nothing to do but get on the boat and take the train from New York, and I'd meet you in Denver.

Act II ✺

Miss ROBERTS.

[*Laughing.*] It's so nice to have someone here to make us laugh.

TOM.

[*A little hurt.*] Oh, I was being serious.

Miss ROBERTS.

[*Seriously.*] Do you really think Colorado would be a good place for a girl like me to go to? A governess!

TOM.

Yes, yes, a girl who has to earn her own living has a better time of it out there than here, more independence, more chance, more life.

Miss ROBERTS.

[*Thoughtfully.*] I do know an English lady in Colorado Springs, at least a great friend of mine does, and I'm sure I could get a letter to her.

TOM.

[*Cheerfully.*] You don't want any letters of introduction; you've got me.

Miss ROBERTS.

[*Smiling.*] Yes, but that is not quite the same thing.

TOM.

No, I suppose not; no, I see: well, can't you write to your friend and tell her to send that letter on at once?

Act II

Miss ROBERTS.

[*Amused.*] You talk as if it were all settled.

TOM.

I wish it were.

Miss ROBERTS.

[*Not noticing that he is flirting with her, she says thoughtfully.*] I wish I knew what to do about leaving here.

TOM.

You told me you had already given my sister notice.

Miss ROBERTS.

She won't take it.

TOM.

She can't make you stay if you want to go.

Miss ROBERTS.

[*Smiling, but serious.*] It's not as simple as that. After Mrs. Baxter has treated me so well, I should be making a poor return, if I left her before she found some one to take my place. On the other hand, my duty to the children is to leave them.

TOM.

A real old-fashioned conscience.

Miss ROBERTS.

One must think of the others.

# Act II

TOM.

It seems to me you're always doing that.

Miss ROBERTS.

If you knew how I sometimes long to be free to do whatever I like just for one day. When I see other girls girls—who don't work for a living—enjoying themselves—it comes over me so dreadfully what I am missing. From the schoolroom window I can see the tennis club, and while I am giving Gladys and Margery their geography lesson, I hear them calling "Play! Fifteen love!" and see the ball flying and the girls in their white dresses, talking to such nice-looking young men.

TOM.

Um, yes. Don't *you* ever talk to any of those nice-looking young men?

Miss ROBERTS.

Of course not.

TOM.

How's that?

Miss ROBERTS.

Governesses never do. We only pass them by as we walk out with the children, or see the backs of their heads in church. Or if we are introduced, as I was to one at the Rectory one day—the occasion is so unusual we feel quite strained and nervous—and can't appear at our best. So that they don't want to pursue the acquaintance even if they could.

Act II

TOM.

You don't seem strained and nervous as you talk to me.

Miss ROBERTS.

[*Innocently.*] You don't seem like the others. [*She meets his eyes—smiles at him and says.*] I must go back to the schoolroom. [*She rises.*]

TOM.

[*Rising and coming to Miss ROBERTS.*] Not yet. Don't go yet. I want you to stay here talking to me. You are sure to hear my little nieces shrieking about in the garden when they have done their cake.

[MRS. BAXTER *enters followed by* MR. BAXTER.]

MRS. BAXTER.

Oh, I hurried back to finish the flowers, but I see you have done them. Thank you.

Miss ROBERTS.

You asked me to do them, Mrs. Baxter.

MRS. BAXTER.

[*Smiling.*] Oh, no, Miss Roberts I think you are mistaken. I only said they were there waiting to be done.

[*She sits in an armchair and begins to read a novel.*]

TOM.

[*In an undertone to* MR. BAXTER.] Have you told her about the picnic?

ACT II ✿

MR. BAXTER.

There was no suitable opportunity so—

TOM.

You're a coward! [*He pushes past him.* TOM *then motions to* MR. BAXTER *to speak to* MRS. BAXTER. *He refuses.* TOM *assuming great cheerfulness, addresses* MRS. BAXTER.] We are all going off on a picnic.

MRS. BAXTER.

[*Pleasantly.*] Oh.

TOM.

Yes. We four and the girls. [*Whispering to* MR. BAXTER.] Back me up.

MR. BAXTER.

[*Rubbing his hands together, and trying to assume jollity.*] Won't that be fun?

MRS. BAXTER.

[*Brightly.*] I think it would be great fun—

TOM.

Ah.

MRS. BAXTER.

—Some day.

TOM.

Why not today?

Act II

MRS. BAXTER.

Why today?

TOM.

[*At a loss for an answer, appeals to* MR. BAXTER *and* Miss ROBERTS.] Why today?

Miss ROBERTS.

In honour of Mr. Kemp's arrival, and it's such a fine day—and—

MRS. BAXTER.

You will find the girls in the schoolroom—dear.

TOM.

[*Very jolly.*] Shall she go and get them ready?

MRS. BAXTER.

[*Innocently.*] What for?

TOM.

The picnic.

MRS. BAXTER.

I thought it had been decided not to go today.

MR. BAXTER.

[*Losing his temper.*] Oh, Dulcie—you know quite well—

Act II

TOM.

[*Signing to* MR. BAXTER *to keep quiet.*] Sh! [*Turning to* MRS. BAXTER *and pretending to make a meek, heartfelt appeal.*] Please let us go today. It's in honour of my arrival. I shall be *so* hurt if I don't have a picnic in honour of my arrival.

MRS. BAXTER.
Suppose it rains.

TOM.
[*At a loss for an answer, appealing to the others.*] Suppose it rains?

Miss ROBERTS.
[*At the window.*] I can't see a single cloud.

MR. BAXTER.
The glass has gone up.

TOM.
It won't rain if we take plenty of umbrellas and mackintoshes and our goloshes.

MRS. BAXTER.
I think we are all too tired.

TOM.
[*Scouting the idea.*] Too tired!

[MR. BAXTER *and* TOM *get together.*]

Act II

MRS. BAXTER.

I suppose it is the excitement of Tom's arrival which is making us feel so next-dayish.

TOM.

Next-dayish!

MRS. BAXTER.

You especially. You were very irritable over the flowers. You ought to go and lie down.

[*She takes up her novel and opens it as if she considered the argument over.* Miss ROBERTS *watches them anxiously.* MR. BAXTER *makes an emphatic gesture, expressing his strong feelings on the subject.*]

TOM.

[*Clutching his arm.*] We *must* keep our tempers. We *must* keep our tempers.

MR. BAXTER.

Shall we poke fun at her?

TOM.

No, no, we'll try a little coaxing first. [*He takes a chair, places it close beside* MRS. BAXTER *and sits. Smiling affectionately at* MRS. BAXTER.] Dear Dulcie.

MRS. BAXTER.

[*Smiling affectionately at* TOM *and patting his knees.*] Dear Tom.

TOM.

We shall have such a merry picnic.

ACT II ❋

MRS. BAXTER.

It *would* have been nice, wouldn't it?

TOM.

Under a canopy of green boughs with the sunbeams dropping patterns on the carpet of moss at our feet.

MRS. BAXTER.

Spiders dropping on our hats.

TOM.

Dear, interesting little creatures, and so industrious.

MRS. BAXTER.

Ants up our arms.

TOM.

[*Laughing*] Lizards up our legs. Frogs in our food. Oh, we shall get back to Nature. [TOM *and* MRS. BAXTER *both laugh heartily both in the greatest good-humour.* MR. BAXTER *and* Miss ROBERTS *also laugh.*] Then it's settled.

MRS. BAXTER.

Yes, dear—it's settled.

TOM.

[*Thinking he has won.*] Ah!

MRS. BAXTER.

We'll all stay quietly at home.

[*She resumes the reading of her book.* TOM *is in dismay.*]

Act II

MR. BAXTER.

The girls will be greatly disappointed.

TOM.

[*With emotion.*] Poor girls! A day in the woods. [*With mock pathos.*] Think what that means to those poor girls.

MRS. BAXTER.

[*Rising and saying seriously to* Miss ROBERTS.] Miss Roberts, you might go to the schoolroom and tell Gladys and Margery that Mamma says they may have a half-holiday and go for a picnic in the woods.

[TOM *winks at* MR. BAXTER. *The three look at each other agreeably surprised.*]

MISS ROBERTS.

[*Moving towards the stairs.*] Thank you. Thank you very much, Mrs. Baxter. I'll go and get them ready at once.

[*She goes out.*]

TOM.

I knew we only had to appeal to her heart.

MR. BAXTER.

We shall want twelve hard-boiled eggs.

TOM.

And some ginger-beer.

MR. BAXTER.

A ham.

Act II

TOM.

A few prawns.

MRS. BAXTER.

[*Looking out of the window to which she has strolled.*] I am glad Miss Roberts and the girls have got such a fine day for their picnic.

[TOM *and* MR. BAXTER *look at each other in dismay.*]

MR. BAXTER.

[*After a pause.*] After leading us on to believe—

TOM.

[*In great good humour.*] Can't you, see she's teasing us? [Going to MRS. BAXTER, he playfully pinches her ear.] Mischievous little puss!

MRS. BAXTER.

[*Gravely to* MR. BAXTER.] Dear, I should like to speak to you.

MR. BAXTER.

Shall we go to my room?

MRS. BAXTER.

I don't see why we need trouble to walk across the hall. [*Glances at* TOM.] We may get this room to ourselves by and by.

[*She sits down.*]

Act II

TOM.

[*Cheerfully taking the hint.*] All right—all right. I'll go and make preparations for the picnic. Don't keep us waiting, Dulcie. Prawns—hams—ginger-beer—

[*He runs off.*]

MR. BAXTER.

[*Slightly peevish.*] I wish you would enter more into the spirit of the picnic. It would do you good to go to a picnic.

MRS. BAXTER.

I don't like the way Tom is carrying on with Miss Roberts. Last evening they monopolized the conversation. This morning—a walk before breakfast. Just now—as soon as my back is turned at it again. I don't like it—and it wouldn't do me any good at all to go to a picnic.

MR. BAXTER.

Tom seems so set on our going.

MRS. BAXTER.

Tom is set on making me go. Tom has taken upon himself to reform my character. He thinks I need stirring up.

MR. BAXTER.

[*Embarrassed.*] What put such an idea as that into your head?

MRS. BAXTER.

[*Looking him straight in the eye.*] The clumsy way you both go about it. [MR. BAXTER *looks exceedingly uncomfortable.*] ... It wouldn't deceive any woman. It wouldn't suit me at all if Tom became interested in Miss Roberts. I could

ACT II

never find another Miss Roberts. She understands my ways so well, I couldn't possibly do without her; not that I'm thinking of myself; I'm thinking only of her good. It's not right for Tom to come here turning her head, and I don't suppose the climate of Colorado would suit her.

MR. BAXTER.

I don't think we need worry yet. They only met yesterday.

MRS. BAXTER.

That is so like you, dear—to sit still and let everything slip past you like the—what was that funny animal Tom mentioned—the mollusc. I prefer to take action. We must speak to Tom.

MR. BAXTER.

You'll only offend him if you say anything to him.

MRS. BAXTER.

I've no intention of saying anything. I think it would come much better from you.

MR. BAXTER.

[*With determination.*] I shan't interfere.

MRS. BAXTER.

[*Trying to work on his feelings.*] It's not often I ask you to do anything for me, and I'm not strong.

MR. BAXTER.

[*Feeling uncomfortable.*] I shouldn't know what to say to Tom, or how to say it.

Act II

MRS. BAXTER

[*Approaching* MR. BAXTER.] You know the way men talk to each other. Go up to him and say, "I say, old fellow, that little governess of ours. Hands off, damn it all." [MRS. BAXTER *nudges* MR. BAXTER *in a masculine way.* MR. BAXTER *laughs and retreats a little.* MRS. BAXTER *is mightily offended.*] I don't consider that trifling with a young girl's affections is food for laughter.

MR. BAXTER.

[*Trying to conceal his amusement.*] I think I'll go and join Tom.

MRS. BAXTER.

Will you tell him we wish him to pay less [Miss ROBERTS *enters.*] attention to—[She sees Miss ROBERTS.]

MR. BAXTER.
We'll see.

[*He goes out.*]

MRS. BAXTER.
I know what that means.

Miss ROBERTS.

[*Coming to* MRS. BAXTER.] If you please, Mrs. Baxter, I'm having such trouble with Gladys and Margery. They want to go to the picnic in their Sunday hats, and I say they must go in their every-day ones.

MRS. BAXTER.

If there's going to be any trouble about the matter, let them have their own way.

Act II ✻

Miss ROBERTS.

Thank you.

[*She is going out.*]

Mrs. BAXTER.

Oh, Miss Roberts. [Miss ROBERTS *stops*.] I want a word with you before you start off on your picnic. Sit down, dear. [Miss ROBERTS *sits down*.] You know how devoted I am to my brother Tom.

Miss ROBERTS.

[*With smiling enthusiasm.*] I don't wonder. He's delightful. So amusing, so easy to get on with.

Mrs. BAXTER.

Yes, but of course we all have our faults, and a man who gets on easily with one will get on easily with another. Always mistrust people who are easy to get on with.

Miss ROBERTS.

[*Solemnly.*] Oh—do you mean he isn't quite honest?

Mrs. BAXTER.

[*Indignantly.*] Nothing of the sort. You mustn't twist my meanings in that manner. You might get me into great trouble.

Miss ROBERTS.

I'm so sorry, but I thought you were warning me against him.

Act II

MRS. BAXTER.

[*Confused.*] Yes—no—yes—and no. [*Recovering herself.*] I am sure you will take what I'm going to say as I mean it, because—[*Smiles at her.*] I am so fond of you. Ever since you came to us I have wished to make you one of the family. When I say one of the family, I mean in the sense of taking your meals with us. Mr. Baxter and the girls and I are so much attached to you. We should like to keep you with us always.

Miss ROBERTS.

I *must* leave at the end of the term.

MRS. BAXTER.

We won't go into all that now.

Miss ROBERTS.

But—

MRS. BAXTER.

[*Smiling and raising her hand in protestation, says politely.*] Try not to interrupt. [*Seriously.*] I should say that a man of Tom's age who has never married would be a confirmed bachelor. He might amuse himself here and there with a pretty girl, but he would never think of any woman seriously.

Miss ROBERTS.

[*Embarrassed.*] I can't think why you are saying this to me.

ACT II

MRS. BAXTER.

[*Plunging at last into her subject.*] To speak quite frankly—as a sister—I find your attitude towards my brother Tom a trifle too encouraging. Last evening, for instance, you monopolized a good deal of the conversation—and this morning you took a walk with him before breakfast—and altogether—[*Very sweetly.*] it looks just a little bit as if you were trying to flirt—doesn't it?

MISS ROBERTS.

[*With suppressed rage.*] I'm not a flirt!

MRS. BAXTER.

I didn't say you were—I said—

MISS ROBERTS.

I'm *not* a flirt—I'm *not*!

MRS. BAXTER.

We'll say no more about it. It was very hard for me to have to speak to you. You have no idea how difficult I found it.

MISS ROBERTS.

Mrs. Baxter, you have often been very kind to me, and I don't want to forget it—but I'd rather not be treated as one of the family any more. I want my meals in the schoolroom, and I mustn't be expected to sit in the drawing-room.

MRS. BAXTER.

Upsetting the whole machinery of the house.

MISS ROBERTS.

I can't go on meeting him at table and everywhere.

Act II

MRS. BAXTER.

I don't see why not.

Miss ROBERTS.

I shouldn't know where to look or what to say.

MRS. BAXTER.

Look out of the window and converse on inanimate objects.

Miss ROBERTS.

[*Mumbles angrily.*] I will not look out of the window and converse on inanimate objects.

MRS. BAXTER.

[*Putting up a warning hand.*] Hush, hush, hush!

Miss ROBERTS.

Please understand I won't be one of the family, and I won't go to the picnic.

[*She goes hurriedly into the garden.*]

MRS. BAXTER.

Oh, oh, naughty girl!

[TOM *and* MR. BAXTER *enter.*]

TOM.

Cook thinks the large basket and the small hamper will suffice. She *said* suffice.

Act II

MRS. BAXTER.

I'm very sorry, Tom, but it is out of the question for us to go to a picnic today.

MR. BAXTER.

Oh, Dulcie.

TOM.

Too late to back out.

MRS. BAXTER.

I haven't backed out. It's Miss Roberts.

TOM.

We can't have a picnic without Miss Roberts.

MR. BAXTER.

What's the matter with her?

MRS. BAXTER.

[*Solemnly.*] Miss Roberts and I have had words. [TOM *whistles quietly.*]

MR. BAXTER.

What about?

MRS. BAXTER.

Never you mind.

Act II

TOM.

Oh, it can't be such a very dreadful quarrel between two such nice sensible women. I guess you were both in the right. [*To* MR. BAXTER.] I guess they were both in the wrong. [*Taking* MRS. BAXTER *by the arm, and cajoling her.*] Come along. Tell us all about it.

MRS. BAXTER.

[*Withdrawing her arm.*] No, Tom, I can't.

TOM.

Then suppose I go to Miss Roberts and get her version.

MRS. BAXTER.

[*In dismay.*] Oh, no, that wouldn't do at all.

TOM.

I only want to make peace. [*To* MR. BAXTER.] Wouldn't it be better if they told me and let me make it up for them?

MR. BAXTER.

Why you?

TOM.

A disinterested person.

MRS. BAXTER.

But you are not.

[*Putting her hand over her mouth.*]

TOM.

[*Turns quickly to* MRS. BAXTER.] What?

Act II •

MRS. BAXTER.

I'm not going to say any more.

[*She sits down.*]

TOM.

[*Seriously.*] You must. If your quarrel concerns me, I have a right to know all about it.

MR. BAXTER.

[*Motioning to* MRS. BAXTER.] You are only putting ideas into their heads.

TOM.

[*Turning sharply on* MR. BAXTER.] Putting what ideas into their heads? [*It dawns upon him what the subject of the quarrel has been.*] Oh! [*To* MRS. BAXTER.] You don't mean to say you spoke to her about—[*He stops embarrassed.*] What have you said to her?

MRS. BAXTER.

I decline to tell you.

TOM.

Then I shall ask her. [*Going.*]

MRS. BAXTER.

[*Quickly.*] No, no, Tom. I—prefer to tell you myself. I spoke very nicely to her. I forget now how the conversation arose, but I think I did say something to the effect that young girls ought to be careful not to have their heads turned by men years older than themselves. [*She looks significantly at* TOM, *who turns away angrily.*] Instead of

Act II

thanking me, she stamped and stormed and was very rude to me—very rude. I simply said [*In a very gentle tone.*], Oh, Miss Roberts! [*Rousing herself as she describes* Miss ROBERTS' *share in the scene.*] But she went on shouting, "I won't go to the picnic, I won't go to the picnic!" and bounced out of the room. It just shows you how you can be deceived in people, and I have been so good to that girl.

TOM.

[*Coming towards* MRS. BAXTER.] I'm very angry—with you—very angry.

MRS. BAXTER.

I simply gave her a word of counsel which she chose to take in the wrong spirit.

TOM.

You interfered. You meddled. It's too bad of you, Dulcie. It's unbearable.

MR. BAXTER.

[*Watching* TOM.] The way you take it any one would think you had fallen in love with our Miss Roberts since yesterday.

MRS. BAXTER.

Yes—wouldn't any one?

TOM.

[*Addressing them both.*] Would there be anything so strange in that? Perhaps I have, I don't know—perhaps as you imply I'm old enough to know better. I don't know. All I know is, I think her the most charming girl I ever met. I've not had time to realize what this is; one must wait and see;

give the seed a chance to produce a flower—not stamp on it. [*To* MRS. BAXTER.] You might have left things alone, when all was going so pleasantly. I was just beginning to think—beginning to feel—wondering if perhaps—later on— Now you've spoilt everything.

MRS. BAXTER.

[*Tearful and angry.*] I won't stay here to be abused. [*Going to the window.*] You've done nothing else all the morning, I'm tired of being taken in hand and improved. No one likes to be improved.

[MRS. BAXTER *goes out through the window.*]

TOM.

I don't want to be unkind to her—but you know how a man feels. He doesn't like any one meddling when he's just beginning to—

MR. BAXTER.

[*Showing embrassment all through the early part of this scene.*] I agree with Dulcie. It would not be suitable for you to marry Miss Roberts.

TOM.

She's as good as any of us.

MR. BAXTER.

[*Hesitatingly.*] It's not that. Miss Roberts from her position here—alone in the world but for us—and having lived here so long—is—in a sense—under my protection.

TOM.

I don't see that, but go on.

Act II

MR. BAXTER.

I feel—in a certain degree—responsible for her. I think it is my duty—and Dulcie's duty—to try and stop her making what we both feel would be an unsuitable marriage.

TOM.

It's a little early to speak of our marriage, but why should it be unsuitable?

MR. BAXTER.

We don't wish her to marry you.

TOM.

Why? Give me a reason.

MR. BAXTER.

Why do you press me for a reason?

TOM.

Because this is very important to me. You have constituted yourself her guardian. I have no objection to *that*, but I want to get at your objection to me as a husband to her. I'm in a position to marry. I'd treat her well if she'd have me. We'd be as happy as the day is long in our little home in the mountains—

MR. BAXTER.

[*Unable to restrain himself.*] You married to her? Oh, no—oh, no, I couldn't bear that.

[*He sinks into a chair and leans his head on his hands.*]

Act II

TOM.

[*Completely taken aback.*] Dick, think what you're saying.

MR. BAXTER.

I couldn't help it. You made me say it—talking of taking her away—right away where I shall never see her again. I couldn't stand my life here without her.

TOM.

Dick, Dick!

MR. BAXTER.

She knows nothing of how I feel; it's only this moment I realized myself what she is to me.

TOM

Then from this moment you ought never to see her again.

MR. BAXTER.

That's impossible!

TOM.

Think of Dulcie, and the girl herself; she can't live in the house with you both now.

MR. BAXTER.

She's lived with us for four years, and no one has ever seen any harm in it; nothing is changed.

TOM.

From the moment you realized what she is to you, everything is changed—

Act II

MR. BAXTER.

There has never been anything to criticize in my conduct to Miss Roberts, and there won't be anything.

TOM.

She is the object of an affection, which you, as a married man, have no right to feel for her. I don't blame you entirely. I blame Dulcie, for throwing you so much together. I remember all you said last evening. Dulcie used to play chess with you, now she tells Miss Roberts to; Dulcie used to go for long walks with you, now she sends Miss Roberts. Out of your forced companionship has sprung this, which she ought to have foreseen.

MR. BAXTER.

Nothing is confessed or understood; I don't see that Miss Roberts is in any danger.

TOM.

She is alone. She has no confidant, no friend, no outlet for the natural desires of youth, for love, for some one to love. She finds you sympathetic—you know the rest.

MR. BAXTER.

It is jealousy that is at the bottom of your morality.

TOM.

It won't do, Dick. It's a most awful state of things.

MR. BAXTER.

If you think that, I wonder you stay here.

ACT II ❂

TOM.

Very well, if you mean I ought to clear out. [*He goes towards the door.*]

MR. BAXTER.

[*Following after* TOM.] No, Tom. Look here, I didn't mean that; but you see, you and I can't discuss this without losing our tempers, so if your visit to us is to continue mutually pleasant, as I hope it will, we'd better avoid the topic in future.

TOM.

Then you mean to keep Miss Roberts here—indefinitely, compromised?

MR. BAXTER.

It's no use going over the ground; we don't see things from the same point of view, so don't let us go on discussing. [*He goes up the stairs and then turns to* TOM.] Tom, you might trust me.

[MR. BAXTER *goes out.*]

[TOM *remains in deep thought, then suddenly makes a determined movement, then stops and sighs.* Miss ROBERTS *enters from the garden. She hesitates timidly when she sees him.*]

MISS ROBERTS.
Mrs. Baxter sent me to get her magazine.

TOM.
Where is my sister?

● ACT II

MISS ROBERTS.

Sitting in the garden. [*She takes up the magazine and is going out again.*]

TOM.

I—[Miss ROBERTS *stops*.] I want to tell you something.

MISS ROBERTS.

I can't stay.

TOM.

I ask you as a great favour to me to hear me.

MISS ROBERTS.

I ought not to stay.

TOM.

I didn't think you'd refuse me when I asked you like that.

MISS ROBERTS.

[*Hesitating.*] I can't stay long.

TOM.

Won't you sit down while I tell you? [*He indicates a chair. Miss ROBERTS comes to the chair and sits.*] I want to tell you about myself, and my life in Colorado.

MISS ROBEBTS.

[*Nervously.*] I don't think I can stay if it's just to talk and hear stories of Colorado.

TOM.

[*Smiling.*] Did you have enough of my stories this morning?

Act II ❋

Miss ROBERTS.

Oh, no, I was quite interested in what you said, but I—

TOM.

You *were* interested. I knew it by your eyes. Why, you even thought you'd like to go there yourself some time.

Miss ROBERTS.

I've changed my mind. I've quite given up that idea now.

TOM.

You'd like it out there. I'm sure you would; it's a friendly country; no one cares who you are, but only what you are, so you soon make friends. That's right. That gives every one a chance, and it's good in this way, it makes a man depend on himself, it teaches him to think clearly and decide quickly; in fact he has to keep wide awake if he wants to succeed. That's the kind of training I've had. I've been from mining camp to mining camp—I've tried my luck in half the camps in California and Colorado. Sometimes it was good, sometimes bad, but take it altogether, I've done well. [*Making the next point clearly and delicately.*] I've got something saved up, and I can always make good money, anywhere west of Chicago. [*Laughing.*] Now I'm talking like a true American; they always begin by telling you how much they've got. You'll forgive me, won't you? It's force of habit. Now what was I saying? [*Seriously.*] We learn to decide quickly in everything; you find me somewhat abrupt; it's only that. I make up my mind all at once, and once it's made up, that's finished—I don't change. [*Hesitating slightly.*] The first time I saw you I made up my mind I said that's the girl for me, that's the girl I want for my wife. [*Leans towards her.*] Will you be my wife?

Act II

Miss ROBERTS.

[*Rising and very much moved and distressed.*] Oh, no, I can't. I didn't know that was coming, or I wouldn't have listened, I wouldn't indeed.

TOM.

[*Following her.*] I've been too abrupt. I warned you I was like that; I make up my mind I want something, and the next thing is, I go straight away and ask for it. That's too quick for you. You want time to think—well, take time to think it over. [Miss ROBERTS *turns to him quickly.*] Don't tell me yet; there's no hurry. I'm not going back for a month or two.

Miss ROBERTS.

I'm very much obliged to you for asking me to marry you, but I can't.

TOM.

Never?

Miss ROBERTS.

No, never! I don't think so.

TOM.

Eh? That sounds like hope.

Miss ROBERTS.

[*Quickly.*] I didn't mean it to sound like hope.

Act II

TOM.

It didn't seem that way last evening when we were talking about the forests and the mountains, and I was telling you how it felt to be back—or this morning when we were getting flowers, or afterwards when we sat here, while they were eating their cake and milk; it seemed to me we were getting on famously.

Miss ROBERTS.

[*Appealingly.*] Oh, please don't go on. I can't bear it. You only distress me. [*She sobs.*]

TOM.

Oh! [*Pausing and looking at her, he sees that she means it and is really distressed.*] I'm sorry.

[*He goes out abruptly.* Miss ROBERTS *is weeping bitterly.* MR. BAXTER *enters. He comes down-stairs towards her and looks down at her with affectionate concern.* Miss ROBERTS *does not notice his presence till he speaks.*]

MR. BAXTER.

What is it?

Miss ROBERTS.

[*Trying to control her sobs.*] Nothing.

MR. BAXTER.

You are in trouble. You are in great trouble—can't you tell me—can't I do anything?

Miss ROBERTS.

No.

Act II

MR. BAXTER.

Wouldn't it do you good to tell somebody? Don't you want some one to tell it all to?

Miss ROBERTS.

I want [*She falters.*]

MR. BAXTER.

What is it you want?

Miss ROBERTS.

I think I want a mother.

[*The effort of saying this brings on her tears afresh; she stands weeping bitterly.* MR. BAXTER *puts his arm about her and draws her gently to him. She yields herself naturally and sobs on his shoulder.* MR. BAXTER *murmurs and soothes her.*]

MR. BAXTER.

Poor child! Poor child! [*While they are in this sentimental position* TOM *and* MRS. BAXTER *appear at the window. They see* MR. BAXTER *and* Miss ROBERTS *but are unseen by them.* Miss ROBERTS *disengages herself from* MR. BAXTER *and goes out sobbing without perceiving* TOM *and* MRS. BAXTER. MR. BAXTER *watches* Miss ROBERTS *off, then turns and see* MRS. BAXTER *for the first time; he becomes very embarrassed under her steady disapproving eyes. To* MRS. BAXTER.] Do you want me to explain?

MRS. BAXTER.

[*Coldly.*] Not at present, thank you, Richard.

ACT II

MR. BAXTER.

I was only—

MRS. BAXTER.

Not now. I prefer to consider my position carefully before expressing my astonishment and indignation.

MR. BAXTER.

Well, if you won't let me explain—

[*He turns to the window and sees* TOM. *He looks appealingly at him.* TOM *ignores him and walks past him.* MR. BAXTER *shrugs his shoulders and goes out through the window.*]

MRS. BAXTER.

I don't know which of them I feel angriest with.

TOM.

Dick, of course.

MRS. BAXTER.

[*Tearfully.*] For thirteen years no man has ever kissed me—except you—and Dick, and Uncle Joe—and Dick's brothers—and old Mr. Redmayne—and the Dean when he came back from the Holy Land. [*Working herself into a rage.*] I'll never speak to Dick again. I'll bundle Miss Roberts out of the house at once.

TOM.

Do it discreetly. Send her away certainly but don't do anything hastily.

ACT II

MRS. BAXTER.

I'm not the woman to put up with that sort of thing.

TOM.

[*Persuasively.*] Don't be hard on her; don't be turning her into the street; make it look as if she were going on a holiday. Pack her off somewhere with the children for a change of air, this afternoon.

MRS. BAXTER.

It's most inconvenient; everything will be upside down. [*Calming herself, she sits in an armchair.*] You're right. I mustn't be too hasty; better wait a few days, till the end of the term, or even till after we come home from the seaside, then pack her off. [*Pause.*] Unless it blows over.

TOM.

[*Astonished and going to her quickly.*] Blows over! It won't blow over while she's in the house. [*Very seriously.*] You're up against a serious crisis. Take warning from what you saw and save your home from ruin. [MRS. BAXTER, *awed and impressed by this, listens attentively.*] You've grown so dependent on Miss Roberts, you've almost let her slip into your place; if you want to keep Dick, you must begin an altogether different life, not tomorrow—[MRS. BAXTER *shakes her head.*] Not next week—[MRS. BAXTER *shakes her head again.*] Now! [MRS. BAXTER's *face betrays her discontent at the unattractive prospect he offers her.*] *You* be his companion, *you* play chess with him, *you* go walks with him, sit up with him in the evenings, get up early in the morning. Be gay and cheerful at the breakfast table. When he goes away, see him off; when he comes home, run to meet him. Learn to do without Miss Roberts, and make him forget her.

Act II

MRS. BAXTER.

Very well. [*Rising*.] She shall leave this house directly—directly I recover.

TOM.

Recover from what?

MRS. BAXTER.

From the shock. Think of the shock I've had; there's sure to be a reaction. I shouldn't wonder if I had a complete collapse. It's beginning already. [*She totters and goes towards staircase.*] Oh, dear, I feel so ill. Please call Miss Roberts.

TOM.

You were going to learn to do without Miss Roberts.

MRS. BAXTER.

That was before I was ill. I can't be ill without Miss Roberts.

[*Puts her hand to her side, turns up her eyes and groans as she totters out.*]

TOM.

Oh! Oh! You Mollusc!

THE CURTAIN FALLS

The Third Act

SCENE. *The same scene one week later. The only difference to the appearance of the room is that there is the addition of an invalid couch with a little table beside it.*

TOM *is in an armchair reading a newspaper.* MISS ROBERTS *comes in carrying two pillows, a scent bottle, and two fans. The pillows she lays on the couch.*

Act III

Miss ROBERTS.

She is coming down today.

TOM.

[*Betraying no interest at all.*] Oh!

Miss ROBERTS.

Aren't you pleased?

TOM.

I think it's about time.

Miss ROBERTS.

How unsympathetic you are—when she has been so ill. For a whole week she has never left her room.

TOM.

And refuses to see a doctor.

Miss ROBERTS.

She says she doesn't think a doctor could do anything for her.

TOM.

Except make her get up. Oh, no! I forgot—it's their business to keep people in bed.

Miss ROBERTS.

You wouldn't talk like that if you'd seen her as I have, lying there day after day, so weak she can only read the lightest literature, and eat the most delicate food.

TOM.

She won't let me in her room.

Act III

MISS ROBERTS.

She won't have any one but Mr. Baxter and me.

TOM.

It's too monstrous. What actually happened that day?

MISS ROBERTS.

Which day?

TOM.

The day you turned me down. [Miss ROBERTS *looks at him troubled. He looks away sadly.*] What happened after that?

MISS ROBERTS.

I was still upset when Mr. Baxter came in and tried to comfort me.

TOM.

[*Grimly.*] I remember.

MISS ROBERTS.

You know he's a kind fatherly little man.

TOM.

Oh—fatherly!

MISS ROBERTS.

Yes, I wept on his shoulder just as if he'd been an old woman.

TOM.

Ah! An old woman! I don't mind that.

Act III

Miss ROBERTS.

Then I went to the schoolroom. Presently in walked Mrs. Baxter. She seemed upset too, for all of a sudden she flopped right over in the rocking-chair.

TOM.

The only comfortable chair in that room.

Miss ROBERTS.

Oh, don't say that. Then I called Mr. Baxter; when he came, she gripped his hand and besought him never to leave her. I was going to leave them alone together, when she gripped my hand and besought me never to leave her either.

TOM.

Did you promise?

Miss ROBERTS.

Of course. I thought she was dying.

TOM.

[*Scouting the idea.*] Dying? What made you think she was dying?

Miss ROBERTS.

She said she was dying.

TOM.

Well, what happened after she gripped you both in her death struggles?

Miss ROBERTS.

We got her to bed, where she has remained ever since.

Act III

TOM.

And here we are a week later, all four of us just where we were, only worse. What's to be done?

Miss ROBERTS.

We must go on as we are for the present.

TOM.

Impossible!

Miss ROBERTS.

Till you go. Then Mr. Baxter and I—

TOM.

More impossible!

Miss ROBERTS.

[*Innocently.*] Poor Mr. Baxter; he will miss you when you go; I shall do my best to comfort him.

TOM.

That's most impossible.

Miss ROBERTS.

He must have some one to take care of him, while his wife is ill.

TOM.

You don't really think she has anything the matter with her?

Miss ROBERTS.

I can't imagine any one who is not ill stopping in bed a week; it must be so boring.

ACT III

TOM.

To a mollusc there is no pleasure like lying in bed feeling strong enough to get up.

Miss ROBERTS.

But it paralyzes everything so. Mr. Baxter can't go to business; I never have an hour to give to the girls; they're running wild and forgetting the little I ever taught them. I can't believe she would cause so much trouble deliberately.

TOM.

Not deliberately, no. It suited Dulcie to be ill, so she kept on telling herself that she was ill till she thought she was, and if we don't look out, she will be. It's all your fault.

Miss ROBERTS.

Oh—how?

TOM.

You make her so comfortable, she'll never recover till you leave her.

Miss ROBERTS.

I've promised never to leave her till she recovers.

TOM.

A death-bed promise isn't binding if the corpse doesn't die.

Miss ROBERTS.

I don't think you quite understand how strongly I feel my obligation to Mrs. Baxter. Four years ago I had almost nothing, and no home; she gave me a home; I can't desert her while she is helpless, and tells me twenty times a day how much she needs me.

Act III

TOM.

She takes advantage of your old-fashioned conscience.

Miss ROBERTS.

I wish she would have a doctor.

TOM.

[*With determination.*] She shall have me.

Miss ROBERTS.

But suppose you treat her for molluscry, and you find out she has a real illness—think how dreadful you would feel.

TOM.

That's what I've been thinking. That's why I've been sitting still doing nothing for a week. I do believe I'm turning into a mollusc again. It's in the air. The house is permeated with molluscular microbes. I'll find out what is the matter with Dulcie today; if it's molluscry I'll treat her for it myself, and if she's ill she shall go to a hospital.

Miss ROBERTS.

[*Going to the bottom of the stairs.*] I think I hear her coming down-stairs. Yes, here she is. Don't be unkind to her.

TOM.

How is one to treat such a woman? I've tried kindness—I've tried roughness—I've tried keeping my temper—I've tried losing it—I've tried the serious tack—and the frivolous tack—there isn't anything else. [*As* MR. *and* MRS. BAXTER *appear.*] Oh! for heaven's sake look at this!

ACT III

[*He takes his paper and sits down, ignoring them both.* MR. BAXTER *is carrying* MRS. BAXTER *in his arms.* MRS. BAXTER *is charmingly dressed as an invalid, in a peignoir and cap with a bow. She appears to be in the best of health, but behaves languidly.*]

MRS. BAXTER.

[*As* MR. BAXTER *carries her down the stairs.*] Take care of the stairs, Dick. Thank you, darling! How kind you are to me. [*Nods and smiles to* Miss ROBERTS.] Dear Miss Roberts! [*To* MR. BAXTER.] I think you'd better put me down, dear—I feel you're giving way. [*He lays her on the sofa.* Miss ROBERTS *arranges the cushions behind her head.*] Thank you—just a little higher with the pillows; and mind you tuck up my toes. [Miss ROBERTS *puts some wraps over her—she nods and smiles at* TOM.] And what have you been doing all this week, Tom?

TOM.

[*Gruffly, without looking up.*] Mollusking.

MRS. BAXTER.

[*Laughs and shakes her hand playfully at* TOM.] How amusing Tom is. I don't understand half his jokes. [*She sinks back on her cushions with a little gasp.*] Oh, dear, how it tires me to come downstairs. I wonder if I ought to have made the effort.

[TOM *laughs harshly.*]

MR. BAXTER.
[*Reprovingly.*] Tom!

Act III

[Miss ROBERTS *also looks reprovingly at* TOM.]

MRS. BAXTER.

Have you no reverence for the sick?

TOM.

You make me sick.

MRS. BAXTER.

Miss Roberts, will you give me my salts, please?

Miss ROBERTS.

They're on the table beside you, Mrs. Baxter.

MRS. BAXTER.

Hand them to me, please. [Miss ROBERTS *picks up the salts where they stand within easy reach of* MRS. BAXTER *if she would only stretch out her hand.* MR. BAXTER *makes an attempt to get the salts.*] Not you, Dick; you stay this side, and hold them to my nose. The bottle is so heavy. [Miss ROBERTS *gives the salts to* MRS. BAXTER, *who gives them to* MR. BAXTER, *who holds them to* MRS. BAXTER'S *nose.*] Delicious!

TOM.

[*Rising quickly and going towards* MRS. BAXTER.] Let me hold it to your nose. I'll make it delicious.

MRS. BAXTER.

[*Briskly.*] No, thank you; take it away, Miss Roberts. I've had all I want.

[*She gives the bottle to* Miss ROBERTS.]

Act III

TOM.

I thought as much.

MRS. BAXTER.

[*Feebly.*] My fan.

MR. BAXTER.

[*Anxiously.*] A fan, Miss Roberts—a fan! [*Miss* ROBERTS *takes a fan and gives it to* MR. BAXTER.]

MRS. BAXTER.

Is there another fan?

MR. BAXTER.

[*Anxiously.*] Another fan, Miss Roberts—another fan!

[*Miss* ROBERTS *gets another fan.*]

MRS. BAXTER.

If you could make the slightest little ruffle of wind on my right temple.

[Miss ROBERTS *stands gently fanning* MRS. BAXTER'S *right temple.* MR. BAXTER *also fans her.* TOM *twists his newspaper into a fan.*]

TOM.

Would you like a ruffle of wind on your left temple?

ACT III ●

MRS. BAXTER.

[Briskly.] No, no—no more fans—take them all away—I'm catching cold. [Miss ROBERTS *takes the fan from* MR. BAXTER *and lays both fans on the table.* MRS. BAXTER *smiles feebly at* MR. BAXTER *and Miss* ROBERTS. TOM *goes back to his chair and sits.*] My dear kind nurses!

Miss ROBERTS.

Is there anything else I can do for you?

MRS. BAXTER.

No, thank you. [*They turn away.*] Yes, hold my hand. [Miss ROBERTS *holds her hand. Then to* MR. BAXTER.] And you hold this one.

[MR. BAXTER *holds* MRS. BAXTER'S *other hand. She closes her eyes.*]

TOM.

Would you like your feet held?

MR. BAXTER.

[*Holding up his hands to silence* TOM.] Hush, she's trying to sleep.

TOM.

[*Going to her says in a hoarse whisper.*] Shall I sing you to sleep?

[MR. BAXTER *pushes* TOM *away.* TOM *resists.*]

Act III

MR. BAXTER.

Come away—she'll be better soon. [*They leave her.*] Oh, Tom, if you knew how I blame myself for this; it's all through me she's been brought so low; ever since the day she caught me comforting Miss Roberts. How she must have suffered, and she's been so sweet about it.

MRS. BAXTER.

[*Opens her eyes.*] I don't feel any better since I came downstairs.

[Miss ROBERTS *comes back to the sofa.*]

MR. BAXTER.

I wish you'd see a doctor.

MRS. BAXTER.

As if a country doctor could diagnose me.

TOM.

Have a baronet from London.

MRS. BAXTER.

Later on, perhaps, unless I get well without.

TOM.

Then you do intend to recover?

MRS. BAXTER.

We hope, with care, that I may be able to get up and go about as usual in a few weeks' time.

Act III ❋

TOM.

When I've gone back to Colorado? [*He pushes* MR. BAXTER *out of the way and approaches* MRS. BAXTER.] I guess you'd be very much obliged to me if I cured you.

MRS. BAXTER.

[*Speaking rapidly and with surprising energy.*] Yes, Tom, of course I should. But I've no confidence in you, and Dr. Ross once said a doctor could do nothing for a patient who had no confidence in him. [*Smiling at* TOM.] I'm so sorry, Tom; I wish I had confidence in you.

TOM.

I have confidence in myself enough for two.

MRS. BAXTER.

Dr. Ross said that wasn't at all the same thing. I wish you'd stand farther off; you make it so airless when you come so close.

[*She waves him off with her hand.*]

TOM.

I'm not going to touch you.

MRS. BAXTER.

[*Relieved.*] Oh, well, that's another matter. I thought you were going to force me up. Try to rather. Do what you like, as long as you don't touch ine or make me drink anything I don't like. I mean that I ought not to have.

Act III

MR. BAXTER.

I wish we could think of some way to make our darling better.

TOM.

I've heard of people who couldn't get up having their beds set on fire.

[*He picks up a box of matches and goes towards* MRS. BAXTER. MR. BAXTER *runs excitedly towards her to shield her.*]

MR. BAXTER.

No, Tom—Miss Roberts!

[Miss ROBERTS *also attempts to shield* MRS. BAXTER.]

MRS. BAXTER.

[*Taking a hand of* MR. BAXTER *and a hand of* Miss ROBERTS—*serenely.*] My dear ones, he doesn't understand—he wouldn't really do it.

TOM.

Wouldn't he? [*He puts the matches back.*]

MRS. BAXTER.

To show him I'm not afraid, leave me alone with him.

TOM.

Going to try and get round me, too? That's no good.

Act III

MRS. BAXTER.

[*Affectionately to* MR. BAXTER *and* Miss ROBERTS.] You need a rest, I'm sure—both of you. Miss Roberts, will you go to the library for me, and change my book?

Miss ROBERTS.

With pleasure.

MRS. BAXTER.

Bring me something that won't tax my brain.

Miss ROBERTS.

[*Soothingly.*] Yes, yes, something trashy—very well.

[*She goes out.*]

MR. BAXTER.

[*Impulsively.*] I need a walk too. I'll go with Miss Roberts. [*About to follow her.*]

MRS. BAXTER.

[*Quickly pulling him back.*] No, you won't, Dick. I want you to go up-stairs and move my furniture. The washstand gets all the sun, so I want the bed where the washstand is, and the wash-stand where the bed is. I wouldn't trouble you, dear, but I don't like to ask the servants to push such heavy weights.

MR. BAXTER.

I'll do anything, dear, to make you more comfortable.

MRS. BAXTER.

Do it quietly, so that I shan't be disturbed by the noise as I lie here. [*Closes her eyes.*]

Act III

MR. BAXTER.

Darling.

[*He kisses her tenderly on the brow, then tiptoes to the stairs motioning* TOM *to keep quiet.* TOM *stamps heavily on the ground with both feet.* MR. BAXTER, *startled, signs to* TOM *to keep quiet then goes out.*]

MRS. BAXTER.

[*Smiling and murmuring.*] Dear Dick!

TOM.

Poor Dick!

MRS. BAXTER.

[*Plaintively.*] Poor Dulcie!

TOM.

Look here, Dulcibella, it's no use trying to get round me. I know you. I've seen you grow up. Why, even in your cradle you'd lie by the hour, gaping at the flies, as if the world contained nothing more important. I used to tickle you, to try and give you a new interest in life, but you never disturbed yourself till bottle time. And afterwards; don't I know every ruse by which you'd make other people run about, when you thought you were playing tennis, standing on the front line, tipping at any ball that came near enough for you to spoil—[*He thumps the cushions.*] and then taking all the credit if your partner won the set. [*Again he thumps the cushions. Each time* MRS. BAXTER *looks startled and attempts to draw them from him.*] And if a ball was lost, would you help to look for it? [TOM *gesticulates* —MRS. BAXTER *watches him in alarm.*] Not

Act III

you. You'd pretend you didn't see where it went. Those were the germs of molluscry in infancy—and this is the logical conclusion—you lying there with a bow in your cap—[*He flicks her cap with his hand.*] having your hands held.

MRS. BAXTER.

[*In an injured tone.*] You have no natural affection.

TOM.

I've a solid, healthy, brotherly affection for you, without a spark of romance.

MRS. BAXTER.

Other people are much kinder to me than you are.

TOM.

Other people only notice that you look pretty and interesting lying there—they wouldn't feel so sorry for you if you were ugly—[MRS. BAXTER *smiles.*] You know that; that's why you stuck that bow in your bonnet. [*He flicks her cap again.*] You can't fool me.

[*Moves away.*]

MRS. BAXTER.

[*Sweetly yet maliciously.*] No, dear, I saw that the morning you made me do the flowers.

TOM.

[*Exasperated at the remembrance of his failure.*] Get up! [*Thumps the table.*]

ACT III

MRS. BAXTER.
I can't get up.

TOM.
Lots of people think every morning that they can't get up, but they do.

MRS. BAXTER.
Lots of people do lots of things I don't.

TOM.
How you can go on like this after what you saw—Dick and Miss Roberts a week ago—after the warning I gave you then. I thought the fundamental instinct in any woman was self-preservation, and that she would make every effort to keep her husband by her. You don't seem to care—to indulge your molluscry you throw those two more and more together.

MRS. BAXTER.
I don't see how you make that out.

TOM.
There they are, both spending the whole of their time waiting on you.

MRS. BAXTER.
In turns—never together—and I always have one or the other with me.

ACT III ❋

TOM.

[*Taking it all in, he laughs and says with admiration and astonishment.*] Oh! Oh! I see. Lie still, hold them both to you and hold them apart. That's clever.

MRS. BAXTER.

Your way was to pack Miss Roberts off; the result would have been that Dick would be sorry for her and blame me. *My* way, Dick is sorry for me, and blames himself, as long as Miss Roberts is here to remind him.

TOM.

You can't keep this game up forever.

MRS. BAXTER.

[*Complacently.*] When I feel comfortable in my mind that the danger has quite blown over—[*She suddenly remembers she is giving herself away too much.*] Oh, but Tom, I hope you don't think I planned all this like a plot, and got ill on purpose?

TOM.

Who knows? It may have been a plot, or suggestions may have arisen like bubbles in the subconscious caverns of your mollusc nature.

MRS. BAXTER.

[*Offended.*] It was bubbles.

Act III

TOM.

You don't know which it was any more than anybody else. Think what this means for the others—there's your husband growing ill with anxiety, neglecting his business—your children running wild when they ought to be at school—Miss Roberts wasting her life in drudgery.

All of them sacrificed so that you may lie back and keep things as they are. But you can't keep things as they are; they'll get worse, unless you get on to yourself and buck up. It's that, or the break up of your home. Now Miss Roberts' presence in the house has ceased to be a danger—[MRS. BAXTER *smiles*.] for the moment. But you wait! Wait till this invalid game is no longer a novelty, and Dick grows tired of being on his best behaviour—or wait till he finds himself in some trouble of his own, then see what happens. He won't turn to you, he'll spare you—he'll turn to his friend, his companion, the woman he has come to rely on—because you shirked your duties on to her, and pushed her into your place. And there you'll be left, lying, out of it, a cypher in your own home.

MRS. BAXTER.

[*Pleasantly.*] Do you know, Tom, I sometimes think you would have made a magnificent public speaker.

> [TOM *is angry. He conveys to the audience by his manner in the next part of the scene that he is trying a change of tactics. He sits.*]

TOM.

I wonder where those two are now?

Act III ✺

MRS. BAXTER.

Miss Roberts has gone to the library, and Dick is up-stairs moving my furniture.

TOM.

[*Gazing up at the ceiling.*] I haven't heard any noise of furniture being moved about.

MRS. BAXTER.

[*Smiling.*] I asked him to do it quietly.

TOM.

Miss Roberts has had more than time to go to the library and back.

MRS. BAXTER.

[*Growing uneasy and sitting up.*] You don't think he's gone too?

TOM.

[*In an offhand way.*] That's what I should do. Pretend to you I was going up-stairs to move furniture, and I should move out after her.

MRS. BAXTER.

It's the first time I've let them out of my sight together since—[*She sits bolt up-right.*] Go and see if they're coming.

[*She points to the window.*]

TOM.

They'd be careful not to be seen from this window.

Act III

MRS. BAXTER.

[*Excitedly.*] They may be in the arbour.

TOM.

It's a very good place.

MRS. BAXTER,

Go and look.

TOM.

I won't.

MRS. BAXTER.

Then I will!

[*She springs off the couch and runs towards the window.*]

TOM.

I thought I should make you get up.

MRS. BAXTER.

[*Brought suddenly to realize what she has done.*] Oh!

TOM.

Now that you are up, better go and look in the arbour.

MRS. BAXTER.

If I do catch them again, of course there will be only one thing for me to do.

TOM.

What's that?

Act III

MRS. BAXTER.

The girls and I must come out and rough it with you in Colorado.

[*She goes out through the window.*]

TOM.

[*Protesting vehemently.*] No, you don't! I won't have that! Not at any price. There's no room for you in Colorado. Oh, dear! What a dreadful thought! [Miss ROBERTS *comes in wearing her hat and carrying the library book in her hand.*] Thank goodness, they were not in the arbour.

Miss ROBERTS.
What?

TOM.
Oh, never mind, never mind.

Miss ROBERTS.
[*Surprised at not seeing* MRS. BAXTER *on the couch.*] Why, where is she?

TOM.
Gone for a chase round the garden.

Miss ROBERTS.
A chase?

TOM.

A wild goose chase. Leave her alone—she needs exercise. You see I was right; she was mollusking.

Act III

Miss ROBERTS.

And she wasn't really ill?

TOM.

[*Quickly.*] Now seize this opportunity to give her notice. Have a plan. Know where you're going to or we shall have —"Dear Miss Roberts stay with us till you find a place"— and the whole thing over again.

Miss ROBERTS.

[*Taking off her hat, says thoughtfully.*] I don't know where I can go at a moment's notice. I suppose you don't actually know of any one in Colorado who wants a governess?

TOM.

No, I can't say I do.

Miss ROBERTS.

Then I suppose it must be the Governesses' Home.

TOM.

[*Kindly.*] We shall hear from you from time to time, I hope?

Miss ROBERTS.

[*Pleased.*] Oh, yes, if you wish to.

TOM.

You'll write sometimes—[Miss ROBERTS *looks up hopefully. But when he says "to my sister" she's disappointed.*] to my sister?

Act III

Miss ROBERTS.

[*Disappointed.*] Oh, yes.

TOM.

And in that way I shall hear of you.

Miss ROBERTS.

[*Sadly.*] If you remember to ask. But people so soon forget, don't they?

TOM.

I shan't forget. I don't want you to forget me.

Miss ROBERTS.

It won't make much difference to you in Colorado whether you're remembered or forgotten by me.

TOM.

I like to know there are people here and there in the world who care what happens to me.

Miss ROBERTS.

[*Faltering.*] That's something, isn't it?

TOM.

It's a real thing to a man who lives out of his own country; we spend a lot of time just thinking of the folks at home.

Miss ROBERTS.

Do you?

Act III

TOM.

[*Looks at her face.*] How young you are—there isn't a line in your face. [*She smiles at him.*] You will let me hear how you get on? [*Moves away.*]

Miss ROBERTS.

[*Disappointed.*] If there's anything to tell. Some people have no history.

TOM.

Yours hasn't begun yet—your life is all before you.

Miss ROBERTS.

A governess's life isn't much.

TOM.

You won't always be a governess. You'll marry a young man, I suppose. I hope he'll be worthy of you.

Miss ROBERTS.

[*Wistfully.*] Would he have to be young for that?

TOM.

It's natural; I suppose it's right—anyway it can't be helped. A man doesn't realize that he's growing old with the rest of the world; he notices that his friends are. He can't see himself so he doesn't notice that he, too—he gets a shock now and then—but ... well, then he gets busy about something else and forgets.

Miss ROBERTS.
Forgets?

Act III

TOM.

Or tries to. I almost wish I'd never come to England. It was easier out there to get busy and forget.

Miss ROBERTS.

You'll find that easy enough when you go back.

TOM.

[*Shaking his head.*] Too much has happened; more than I can forget. But I must buck up because I have to be jolly as a duty to my neighbours, and then your letters—they'll cheer me. And when that inevitable letter arrives to tell me you've found happiness, I shall send you my kindest thoughts and best wishes, and try not to curse the young devil whoever he is. So you see we can always be friends, can't we? In spite of the blunder I made a week ago. Don't quite forget me—[*Taking her hands and shaking them.*] when he comes along.

[*He goes and sits on the couch disconsolately.*]

Miss ROBERTS.

Shall I tell you something?

TOM.

What?

Miss ROBERTS.

Oh, no—I can't!

TOM.

You must now you've begun.

Act III

MISS ROBERTS.

I daren't.

TOM.

I want you to.

MISS ROBERTS.

Well, don't look at me.

TOM.

I'm ready.

[*He looks at her, and then turns his back to her.*]

MISS ROBERTS.

Suppose there was a girl, quite young, and not bad looking, and she knew that her chief value as a person was her looks and her youth, and a man oh, I don't know how to say this—

TOM.

I'm not looking.

MISS ROBERTS.

He had great value as a person. He was kind and sensible, and brave, and he had done things. He wasn't young, but he couldn't have lived and still had a smooth face, so she liked him all the better for not having a smooth face—his face meant things to a girl, and if he wanted to give her so much—such great things—don't you think she'd be proud to give him her one little possession, her looks and her youth?

Act III

TOM.

You don't mean us? [*He turns to her.*]

MISS ROBERTS.

[*Overcome with confusion.*] Don't look at me. I'm ashamed. [*Covers her face with her hands.* TOM *goes to her, gently draws her hands from her face and holds them both in his.*] I wouldn't have dared to tell you only I couldn't let you go on thinking what you were thinking. When you asked me to marry you a week ago and I said "No"—it was only because I was so hurt—my pride was hurt and I thought —oh, never mind now—I wanted to say "Yes" all the time.

TOM.

[*Looking at her and saying to himself, as if he scarcely believed it.*] I am really going to take her with me to Colorado.

[*Kisses her. After a slight pause*, MR. BAXTER *enters limping painfully.*]

MR. BAXTER.

I've sprained my ankle—moving that wash-stand.

TOM.

Oh, my poor old chap—what can we do for you?

MISS ROBERTS.

You ought to have some lint and a bandage. [*To* TOM.] You'll find it in a cupboard in the spare room—your room.

TOM.

All right—hold on while I go and get it. [*He puts* MR. BAXTER'S *hand on the post of the stairs; then he goes out.*]

Act III

MISS ROBERTS.

Hold on to me, Mr. Baxter.

[*She supports him.* MRS. BAXTER *enters from the garden without seeing* MR. BAXTER *and* Miss ROBERTS.]

MRS. BAXTER.

They're not in the arbour. [*Catching sight of them.*] What, again?

MISS ROBERTS.

He's sprained his ankle.

MRS. BAXTER.

[*Rushing to him.*] Sprained his ankle—oh, my poor Dick!

MR. BAXTER.

[*Looking surprised at* MRS. BAXTER.] What, you up—running about?

MRS. BAXTER.

I've taken a sudden turn for the better.

MR. BAXTER.

[*Mournfully.*] I wish you'd taken it a bit sooner; making me move that damned, old wash-stand. [*Then suddenly.*] Oh, my foot!

MRS. BAXTER.

Let me help you to my couch.

[*Tom comes in with bandages.*]

Act III ❋

MR. BAXTER.

You wouldn't know how. [*Pushes her away.* MRS. BAXTER *gives an exclamation of horror. Turning to* Miss ROBERTS.] Miss Roberts!

MRS. BAXTER.

Let me!

MR. BAXTER.

No, no—not now. [*As* Miss ROBERTS *assists him to the sofa.*] You see, she's used to helping people, and you're not.

[Miss ROBERTS *kneels and begins to un-tie his shoe-lace.*]

MRS. BAXTER.

[*To* TOM.] He refuses my help.

TOM.

He turns to the woman he has come to rely on. Now is your chance. Seize it; you may never get another.

MR. BAXTER.

I want a pillow for my foot.

MISS ROBERTS.

[*Rising.*] A pillow for your foot?

TOM.

[*To* MRS. BAXTER.] Go on—go on—get it.

Act III

MRS. BAXTER.

[*Running for the pillow.*] A pillow for his foot. [*She anticipates* Miss ROBERTS, *snatches the pillow and brings it to* MR. BAXTER, *then looking indignantly at* Miss ROBERTS *she raises* MR. BAXTER'S *sprained foot with one hand as she places the pillow under it with the other.* MR. BAXTER *utters a yell of pain.*] Oh, my poor Dick, I'm so sorry. Did I hurt you?

MR. BAXTER.

[*Looking at her in wonder.*] Why, Dulcie, but it seems all wrong for me to be lying here, while you wait on me.

MRS. BAXTER.

I want you to rely on me, dear, so that when you're in trouble, you'll turn to me. What can I do for your poor foot? We must get some—some—

TOM.

Bandages.

[*Throwing bandages to* MRS. BAXTER.]

MRS. BAXTER.

Yes, and some—some arnica. Miss Roberts never thought of arnica.

MISS ROBERTS.

I'll go and look for it. [*She makes a slight movement.*]

Act III

MRS. BAXTER.

[*Pleasantly.*] Don't trouble, Miss Roberts, I will go myself directly. [*Then to* MR. BAXTER.] You know, dear, we must learn to do without Miss Roberts.

TOM.

You'll have to. She's coming back to Colorado with me.

MRS. BAXTER.

[*Going to* Miss ROBERTS.] Tom, this is news. Dear Miss Roberts, I'm so glad.

MR. BAXTER.

[*Holding out his hand to* TOM.] So am I. [TOM *shakes hands with* MR. BAXTER.]

MRS. BAXTER.

But oh, how we shall miss you.

Miss ROBERTS.

I hope I'm not being selfish!

MRS. BAXTER.

Oh, no, no, dear. I'm glad you're going to make Tom happy. We shall do very well here; it's high time the children went to school. I've been thinking about it for a long time. [*She kneels by* MR. BAXTER.] And now that I'm so much better, I shall be able to do more for my husband, play chess with him—go walks with him—Tom shall never have another chance to call me a mollusc.

Act III

TOM.
Bravo! Bravo!

MR. BAXTER.
Dulcie!

MRS. BAXTER.
Dearest!

Miss ROBERTS.
[*To* TOM.] You've worked a miracle!

TOM.
[*Quietly to* Miss ROBERTS.] Were those miracles permanent cures? [*Shakes his head.*] We're never told! We're never told!

THE END

Afterword
by Hugh Walpole[1]

I

HUBERT HENRY DAVIES WAS BORN on the 30th March 1869 at Woodley in Cheshire. He was the fourth child of William Henry and Martha Davies. William Henry Davies came of a long line of Welsh Nonconformist divines and was born at Ludlow, on the Shropshire border of Wales, in the year 1837. It would probably have been difficult to find any more remarkable survival of primitive Puritanism down the generations than that instanced by Will Davies and his ancestors. Since the days before the Commonwealth they had held fast their faith, permitting no development in respect either of its precept or its practice; and in matters of doctrine and Sabbath observance Will Davies, at the end of the nineteenth century, saw eye to eye with the forefather who had been shot at in his Welsh pulpit for preaching Nonconformity at the beginning of the seventeenth. The problem for the student of heredity is—how did the writer of some of the gayest comedies in the English language come to grow on so stiff and uncompromising a stock?

But though Hubert Henry's early environment was entailed upon him by the stern tradition of his father,

---

[1] From the original Introduction to *The Plays of Hubert Henry Davies*, London, 1921.

❖ Afterword

he was by temperament much more akin to his mother. Martha Davies's father had begun life as a workman in an iron-foundry at Hyde in Cheshire, but having a strain of inventiveness in him he lifted himself out of this laborious level, dying in early middle age the master of his own ironworks. His wife, who came from the same humble class as himself, worked in her girlhood at a neighbouring cotton mill, only quitting her spindles the day before her marriage. From these parents Martha inherited a natural simplicity and dignity of character; and without being in the least intellectual she was endowed with a fine and quick perception to which a temper was given by the admirable education which her father contrived for her. She suffered from great physical weakness almost all her life, and this, together with the rigid home discipline imposed by her husband, severely restricted both her own life and that of her young children.

The first years of young Hubert's life were spent in a smoky suburb of Manchester, where the distance was everywhere shut out by bricks and mortar and where the sky overhead was never clear. In those early days his only form of outdoor sport was running or walking on cinder roads and stone pavements, and his only contact with nature was the tending of a sycamore sapling and a monkey-flower plant that grew in the tiny plot of earth apportioned to him in the dreary back garden. When he was eight years old his family removed to Wilmslow, a Cheshire village some twelve miles from Manchester. Here for a space he knew the freedom of green fields and wide skies; and it was during these impressionable years of his boyhood that he unconsciously absorbed the atmosphere that later on characterised his comedies of simple domestic life. Not that the people in his plays were ever drawn direct from life; there is nowhere

Afterword

in his characterisation anything approaching to portraiture, though it may be noted in passing that the majority of the names he gave to his characters were locally familiar to him in the Wilmslow days. When he had reached the age of eleven he was sent to a little school in the village as preparatory to the Grammar School in Manchester, whither he soon departed; but in 1886, the father's affairs having become seriously involved, the family went back again to live in Manchester, and at the age of seventeen Hubert was taken from school and put into business.

The story of his life could be told in very few lines. Outwardly it was singularly uneventful and devoid of incident, but between the end of his school days and the beginning of his success as a dramatist he lived through years of very intense subjective drama—drama that was by no means chiefly comedy. During the long slow-moving time of boyhood his life had been a happy, humdrum affair enough, and the glamour of his own vivid vitality and imagination hid from him the extreme narrowness of his environment; but when youth came, quickening all the springs of his being and opening the eyes of his self-consciousness, he began to be aware of the larger possibilities which life contained, and thenceforward his soul entered into rebellion against the cramping traditions of his lot. When the time came for him to be broken into business he was, by a strangely unhappy prompting, put into his father's office to undergo the process. He had made no especial mark while at school and he now shone still less at business. He had not yet formed any definite idea of being a writer, but the whole atmosphere of commerce was utterly distasteful to him, and he never at any time in his life attempted to assume an interest in things which he did not feel. Nonchalance towards the processes of calico-printing on the part of a beginner was, naturally enough, very trying to his father, to whom a manner of business-like alertness was a matter of conscience rather than of temperament, and the relationship between father and son, never at any time a close or sympathetic one, began under the daily friction of office life to grow more strained and critical.

The vein of religious melancholy which Will Davies, the father, had inherited from his Welsh ancestors was, under stress of accumulating misfortune, developing into a state of morbid spiritual nervousness, which reacted upon his family in innumerable little acts of interference and discipline. While his children were in the stage of unthinking infancy his carefulness and kindness towards them had been never-failing, but as they grew to years of reason and began to form opinions of their own he failed to understand them or sympathise with them, and where he could not understand he knew no other way than to coerce and forbid. What this constant criticism and repression must have cost to a generous, sensitive temperament like Hubert's it is impossible to estimate. It was the clash of two diametrically opposed systems and temperaments; and both father and son suffered painfully from its effects. But though, as always in such cases, it was the younger and more ardent who received the deepest hurt, in later life Hubert had come to the belief that no man can fairly be blamed for having a narrow mind any more than for having a narrow chest, and after he had achieved his full liberation it is certain that all the personal bitterness had died out of his early memories.

Both at home and in the office these years were for Hubert full of deep difficulty and depression; his relations with his mother and his brother and his sisters were, however, so happy and intimate that they lightened all this period, and it is unquestionably true that it was just the

Afterword

stern experiences of this time that taught him concentration and self-discipline.

It was when he was about twenty that he first formed the determination to be a dramatist, and thenceforward nothing ever shook his conviction that he was going to be a successful one. The first time that he had ever been inside a theatre was one summer when at the age of fourteen he had gone from Wilmslow to visit some elderly relatives in London. He stayed in Camden Square and was taken to the Adelphi Theatre to see *The Streets of London*, and the performance in that play of Miss Clara Jecks in the part of the Cockney boy Dan filled him with the keenest delight. But this was in London, and when later on at home in Manchester he went to the play there were great heart-burnings about it. His father's habitual attitude towards even the most innocent forms of amusement had then become one of pained and solemn disapproval, and it will readily be understood, therefore, that the theatre called forth his severest reprobation. There were many painful scenes between them about it, conducted in a sombre tragedy strain; and when on the occasion of one of Henry Irving and Ellen Terry's rare visits to Manchester Hubert persisted, in spite of the parental displeasure, in going to see them in *The Merchant of Venice* all Will's Welsh ancestry rose up indignantly within him and he threatened his son with expulsion from the home.

Nevertheless, Hubert now never for a moment desisted from his ambition, and summer or winter, week-day or Sunday, it was only at the end of the evening, after the usual good-nights had been said, that, mounting the creaking little stair to the top of the house, he began the real work of the day. Whether the evening had been spent at home or away, whether he went upstairs early or late, scarcely an evening passed at that time that he did not sit for hours at

Afterword

an old dressing-table in the attic, surrounded by the family's dusty travelling trunks, writing pieces long and short, tragic and comic, while the family slept below and the street outside grew silent and empty. Side by side with his writing he had now also become a close student of modern play construction, both French and English. He was probably in those days more influenced by the construction of Pinero than by that of any other English dramatist, and among contemporary French writers, by the work of Scribe and Sardou. He read widely the plays of the period, Ibsen, Wilde, Sudermann, Maeterlinck, all had their turn. Also the older English writers—Goldsmith and Sheridan, the dramatists of the Restoration, and the Elizabethans both great and small.

Doubtless those early efforts were no less artificial and derived than the experimental work of most young writers. His manuscripts. when completed came back to him with painful regularity from the actors and managers to whom they had been sent; but though disappointments were many and bitter, and though he had not a single friend at hand to advise him as to the best method of pursuing his end, he never for an instant lost the belief that he would one day succeed, and when a note of praise and encouragement came one day from Mrs. Kendal, he walked to business on air for a week afterwards even though she had at the same time returned his MS. He nevertheless perceived that he was now in a back-water, that the years were passing swiftly by and that he was achieving nothing. He had an uncle who in early life had gone forth to seek his fortune in the New World and had prospered exceedingly, not only in the group of islands in the Pacific, where he had his headquarters, but also on the mainland of America. To this uncle now living in England Hubert, in the summer of 1893, went for advice; the uncle was practical and encouraging, and by his generosity it

Afterword

was arranged there and then that Hubert should go out to America in the following September with a sufficient sum of money in his pocket to live on for three months, thus giving him time to look round for employment. If at the end of that time he had been unsuccessful in making any connections for himself, his uncle undertook to find him a post in San Francisco in a large shipping office there allied to his own firm. On the 16th September 1893 he sailed from Liverpool in the S.S. *Campania* in company with his uncle and two cousins.

I will pass swiftly over his American experiences. He stayed for the rest of that year in Chicago and sought everywhere for a situation, tried to get work on various papers, made many efforts and many false hopes and starts but no success. In April of the next year he reached San Francisco and at once began work in the office of Messrs. Williams Dimond, shippers. In May of 1898 he had his first play produced, a one-act piece entitled *A Dream of Love*, part dialogue, part pantomime; it was written for and acted by Madame Pilar-Morin, a French pantomimist, and was produced by her at the Orpheum, San Francisco. He had good press notices but no striking success with the public. It was just at this time that his Uncle Theo Davies died and he left Hubert £1000, which, while not immediately altering his plans, gave him the all-important breathing-space for play-writing. During the next few months he stayed on in San Francisco at the office, continually writing and occasionally contributing short stories, poems, and articles to various San Francisco papers, "The Lotus," "Philistine," etc. Then in October 1897 he was appointed musical and dramatic critic to the News Letter, a San Francisco weekly, and on the last day of that year he left the office for ever to devote himself entirely to journalism and literature.

● Afterword

In March of 1899 he received an offer from Daniel Frohman to produce *The Weldons*, a drama in four acts which Hubert had completed in the previous autumn, for a single performance at the Empire Theatre, New York. This decided Hubert to leave San Francisco at once for New York. He attended the last week's rehearsals, and the public performance on April 6 had a good reception and encouraging notices but was never afterwards revived. He then paid a short visit to England, returned to America in September, settling this time in New York, where he stayed two years. His history henceforward is the history of his plays.

In March of 1900 a one-act piece. *Fifty Years Ago*, was successfully produced by Miss Lilian Burkhart. She opened at Omaha and toured the States with it. The rest of the year he was hard at work, chiefly on a play that Daniel Frohman had asked him to write. This was *Cynthia*, which, however, did not satisfy Frohman. He spent the earlier part of 1901 in New York writing notably *Mrs. Gorringe's Necklace*. Then he left America for good and spent the summer with his family in Shropshire, where he wrote most of *Cousin Kate*. Then in the autumn he came to London and settled in the Royal Avenue, Chelsea. 1902 was his fateful year. In the spring *Cousin Kate* was submitted to Frederick Harrison and Cyril Maude. They accepted it immediately as it stood and made a contract to produce it within twelve months. In October he read *Mrs. Gorringe's Necklace* to Charles Wyndham and Mary Moore. They closed with it at once, made a contract, and promised to produce it as early in the following year as possible.

Mrs. Gorringe's Necklace had its first production May 12, 1903, and it was at once an immense success. This was followed in the same year by the appearance on June 18 of

Afterword

Cousin Kate, another most successful play. The dates of the production of his other plays were as follows :

Cynthia ... May 16, 1904
(produced in New York, March 16, 1903).
Captain Drew on Leave ... October 24, 1905,
The Mollusc ... October 15, 1907.
Lady Epping's Lawsuit October 12, 1908.
Bevis ... April 1, 1909.
A Single Man ... November 8, 1910.
Doormats ... October 3, 1912.
Outcast ... September 1914.

After the production of *Outcast* he went to France and did notable work in the hospitals of Paris and elsewhere. In the following year, however, he had a bad nervous breakdown, and after a long and trying illness he died, as truly a willing victim in the cause of his country as any soldier in France, on August 17, 1917.

II

SUCH ARE THE BARE FACTS OF DAVIES'S LIFE. When one comes to an attempt at estimating his character and personality, one is faced with a real difficulty. Of all the notable figures in that pre-war London, now so rapidly becoming traditional and even romantic, Davies was the very last to wear his heart on his sleeve. On the very first five minutes of that now famous premiere of *Mrs. Gorringe's Necklace* a certain attitude was forced upon Davies from the outside. He was the recognised jester of that pre-war London world; there is

Afterword

nothing that human nature likes better than the emphasising of little foibles, weaknesses, and oddities by some observer who has not too acid or malicious a touch. Best of all is the satirist of human society who at the same time satirises himself. With him we feel absolutely safe, and although he may laugh at us, we are secure from treachery because he is target with ourselves.

It was just this position that Davies occupied. Those early years of stem discipline and dreary surroundings had trained him to snatch fun wherever he found it. He could see nothing, hear nothing, share in nothing without finding something that made life more entertaining, more whimsical, more delicately absurd than it had been before, and so delighted was he with his little discoveries that he must share them with his friends, and those friends, finding that to them also life was suddenly more entertaining and whimsical, delighted in his company, demanded that he should be forever at his best, and in many cases refused to see him in any other role but the one that he so beautifully filled. Again and again, watching him, I used to wonder that he could so buoyantly keep it up. I used to wonder still more that he could find certain people, who seemed to all the rest of the world tiresome and heavy, such excellent company. His wit was quick, clean, darting, always sure of its aim, always knowing when to stop, always kindly and, best of all, original. The pageant of London entertained him unceasingly, and although he loved Italy and enjoyed his visits to America, it was London that was his real hunting ground. He was able to say the obvious things about people and places without ever being obvious at all, giving his point of view a sudden little twist which made it entirely his own, a point of view generally a little kinder than the others, and always a little neater. He showed that characteristic so

Afterword

frequently seen in those who have had dull and restricted childhoods, of a perpetual pleasure in the tiniest adventures that life brought to him. It was not that he marvelled at his own success, because, as I have already said, he had from the very beginning determined to succeed, but the things that success brought to him were always twice as delightful as he had expected them to be. People were more amusing, places more beautiful, books and pictures and travel more entrancing, the London bustle more entertaining than he had ever dreamt that he would find them, and one of the things that made his company so perpetually refreshing was the sensation that one had with him that today was the first day and the last day, there had never been any day like it before, that there would never be any day like it again, and that therefore one must live every moment of it. He had the actual consciousness of his happiness at the instant that he was experiencing it, and that is perhaps one of the rarest gifts given to human beings. Behind his fun and happiness one always had the sense of the artist at work. Not that he was deliberately using everything that came to him as material for future plays, but rather that he took the things—a little dinner party, a first night, a ride on an omnibus, luncheon at the Garrick Club, an interview in the middle of Piccadilly with an old gentleman who had just lost his dog and was very unhappy about it, a visit to Madame Tussaud's, a ride in a taxi on a summer's evening out to Harrow—whatever it might be—and made them little rounded episodes coloured and decorated with his fantasy and humour, and then left them there for you to enjoy so that they remain forever afterwards as something distinct and framed, hanging upon the wall of your mind so long as your house should endure.

His brother describes him when he was eight years old as "a chubby, pink-faced child, with bright yellow hair, his busy

Afterword

figure a familiar object in the country, playing rounders in the hayfield, catching frogs in the pond, bustling in and out of the stables and shippons of the neighbouring farm in order to investigate the mystery of the birth of calves and foals and the death of pigs, a cheerful, laughter-loving creature though somewhat easily moved to scorn and disrespect of elders." That description might remain almost true of him to the very outbreak of the war. He stayed incredibly young, and I have often seen on his face exactly that look of an inquiring child in whose mind some small roguery is plotting, an expression humorous, a little malicious, entirely engaging, breaking into laughter at the earliest possible moment. It was in this particular character that he was known to most of his contemporaries. Where Davies was there would be sure to be fun, games different from any other games, points of view that never did any harm and made the heaviest bore entertaining. It was natural that he should be wanted everywhere and superficially he seemed to give himself up to that life of amusement and light-hearted laughter. His own family and one or two of his most intimate friends knew that underneath there was quite another Hubert Henry. He was himself desperately shy of his deeper side. This shyness came, I used to think, from an innate modesty and his vision of himself as some one of a small, cheerful talent who had no right to bother the rest of the world with his real feelings about life. He approached his friends with an attitude of easy comradeship and lighthearted fun, and it was not until they had enjoyed his friendship for some time that they realised his unswerving loyalty, his immediate unselfishness if they made any demands upon him, his extraordinary wisdom and common sense when they were in trouble. They never made any appeal to him that he refused. He never forgot an obligation that he owed. When he chose to speak seriously of literature and art and music, you were surprised

Afterword

to discover how quietly and without any self-intrusion he had been working and developing his own line of study as consistently as though he had no social existence at all.

After the success of his earlier comedies, he was determined to prove to the world his ability to write plays of a much more serious kind, and in the first half of *Outcast* he undoubtedly did this. Had the war not smashed in upon the world, we would have seen, I am convinced, quite a new development in his art, but the war did come and it killed him. His attitude of fun and humorous observation of life had never hidden from his friends his deep tenderness of heart. He simply could not bear that people should suffer and be unhappy. Until the war he had the sense that human beings on the whole got enough out of life to make it worthwhile for them, and although there was unhappiness and misery there was sufficient love and laughter and beauty to make the world go round. During the early months of the war, when he was doing his hospital work in France, he still felt the impulse of courage and unselfishness that those first weeks of August 1914 brought so magnificently forward. Then as the months went on, as the war so hopelessly lengthened, as he saw in those same hospitals the pain and the agony, the frustrated hopes, and the lingering deaths, he began to feel, I think, that the whole of his earlier estimate of life was wrong and that the world was a hideous place into which he had been somehow tricked in believing. He was now forty-five years of age and it all must suddenly have seemed to him too vast and terrible for anyone to deal with. He violently overworked his strength, broke down in health, came home, and then for two years struggled to secure again some of his earlier vitality and confidence; but his heart was too tender, his imagination too keen. I remember in the second or third year of the war, when I was home on leave, paying him a visit in Oxford. He had just

Afterword

read a book of mine that had for its background the Russian Front in Galicia. I remember how he spoke with a sort of feverish urgency as though he wanted to drive everybody together to stop the horrible massacre at the earliest possible moment, and then suddenly, with a little broken gesture, cried, "And here am I in Oxford doing nothing to help to stop it. Nothing at all." The war overwhelmed him so dreadfully that he could not think of his plays, he could get no theme that did not seem to him unspeakably trivial, he despised himself and his art and his earlier view of life with a contempt that those things never for a moment deserved and that had been fed by the working of his imagination ceaselessly upon the miseries and tragedies of the war. He did literally die of a broken heart. He loved his fellow-beings too deeply to endure the thought of their great unhappiness, and he was too immediately conscious of their suffering to look forward to the day when the world would recover from its sickness and men be brothers once again. To so many of us looking back he will always stand out as the happiest, freest, kindest, and warmest-hearted of all the figures in that pre-war London. Nobody since has seemed to have quite that mixture of childlike simplicity, wise common sense, burning generosity, and unfaltering loyalty. He remains a whimsical, laughing knight-errant, and there is no one like him anymore.

III

ANY CONSIDERATION OF THE PLAYS of Hubert Henry Davies must lead at least to one inevitable conclusion about them and that is their timelessness. There is perhaps no form of art that dates quite so decisively as the play of social

AFTERWORD

manners, and it is only when, as in *The Way of the World* and *The School for Scandal*, the motives of the human beings concerned are universal and not of a period that the play has any chance of survival with a fresh generation. Davies had this at least in common with Sheridan, that every one of his plays contains one or two scenes built on the pathos and humour of characteristics that are eternally in human nature, and it is because of these little scenes that his work will live. When one considers them—-the losing of Mrs. Gorringe's necklace, "the tea a deux" in *Cousin Kate*, the little meal with the typist in *A Single Man*, the breakfast scene in *Doormats*, the knitting scene in *Captain Drew*, and every scene from first to last in *The Mollusc*—these are the things that bring Davies into the true line of English writers of comedy in full and rightful succession to Wycherley, Congreve, Sheridan, and Wilde. These scenes are often, let it at once be confessed, placed in a setting unworthy of them. A dramatist who sees human nature as human nature is and wishes to put upon the boards truthfully what he sees has a difficulty of construction and development that a writer who is thinking first and foremost of the stage and the stage world cannot feel. In our own time we have seen two schools of the drama abruptly diverge. We have allowed our realists, St. John Ervine, Lennox Robinson, and others, to give us real life as they see it, however slender the theme upon which they hang their pictures. Many of our other dramatists have quite frankly sacrificed human nature to dramatic effect, and we have understood from the beginning of their plays that they are going to do this and have accepted their convention. It is a noteworthy illustration of this that the one play of John Galsworthy that has been a real popular success departs further from real human nature than any other that he has written.

Afterword

Davies in those years before the war must have felt that difficulty less sharply than the dramatists of today. Bernard Shaw and Hankin were almost alone at that time in their determination to write of life as they saw it, and to sacrifice all the dramatic conventions at once if by doing so they could tell the truth. In Davies's very first success, *Mrs. Gorringe's Necklace*, this struggle between real life and the life of the theatre was apparent. Listen to Mrs. Gorringe, who has just lost her necklace and is explaining to a detective how she lost it.

JERNIGAN.

And now how did you come to discover the diamonds were missing?

MRS. GORRINGE.

Well, I Went up to my room when I came in from the polo match, and suppose the dressing-table to be there —[*points to* VICKY] where Miss Jardine is. And the door where this one is. [*Points to the door.*] I came in at the door something like this. [*Goes to the door, opens it, goes just outside and comes in again.*] I closed the door. [*Closes the door and goes towards* VICKY *as she says.*] Then I crossed over to the dressing-table in quite an ordinary manner, just as I am doing now. [*When she has nearly arrived at* VICKY *she stops suddenly.*] Oh, no. I've made a mistake. The dressing-table, of course, would be there. [*Points towards* MRS. JARDINE.) I was thinking of the one at home. [*She pauses a moment undecided, then says.*] I must come in again. [*She then runs to the door, opens it, goes just outside, closes it, opens it again and puts her head just inside to say.*] Now you are to suppose I didn't come in before. [*Takes her head back and closes the door.*]

Afterword

MRS. JARDINE

[*scarcely able to restrain her impatience*], I shall scream in a minute.

MRS. GORRINGE.

I crossed over to the dressing-table—which, of course, is here now. [*Points to a spot near* Mrs. JARDINE, *walks towards it, and stands still.*] I opened my jewel-case. I don't know what made me do that then. I suppose I must have had a presentiment. Oh, no. It was to get these rings. [*Bends up her hand to show her rings.*] I thought it looked different somehow, and what was it I said to myself? [*Frowns as she thinks a moment.*] Oh, yes. I remember saying to myself, "Well, that's funny ! " Then all at once it came across me like a flash of lightning, and I clasped my hands and exclaimed [*clasps her hands dramatically*], "Great Heavens, my diamond necklace has gone !" [*Drops her dramatic pose and tone.*] Just like that.

Contrast with that the following scene in the same play when the young villain of the piece confesses to the noble elderly friend that he has committed the theft.

DAVID.

I know I'm unworthy of her, but— I'm not all bad.

MOWBRAY.

I know that. I don't ask you to be perfect. We all have our faults. But it isn't the number of his sins that mark a man—it's the kind.

DAVID

[*humbly*]. Don't you think—with this experience—I can be different?

MOWBRAY.

The curse of degeneracy is always there, in your mind and in your heart. It's like a taint in the blood. It warps your judgment, poisons your impulses, lures you into constant danger.

DAVID.

But with Isabel to help me —

MOWBRAY.

To help *you*—she—to give up *her* life to *you* will bring her only shame and sorrow—to expose *her* sweet nature day after day to *your* contamination — to make her the mother of *your* children. No, it's not to be thought of—you must not marry her.

DAVID.

I can't give her up.

MOWBRAY.

Then she must know the truth. If you don't break your engagement before you leave this house I shall tell her that—

ISABEL

[*Calls outside*]. David!

Is not the one quotation as true to real life as the other is true to the life of the theatre? He was never again to blend so crudely the two elements as he did in *Mrs. Gorringe*, but he found it always, I think, exceedingly difficult to find a fable which would be interesting enough dramatically without driving him from the work that he really loved. Once in *The Mollusc* he was entirely successful, and in *Cousin Kate* he almost succeeded, but he gravely endangered what is to myself his very best play. *Captain Drew on Leave*, by the old

Afterword

theatrical scene of the woman going to the man's rooms at night, there to be discovered by man No. 2, and in his less successful plays, Bevis, *A Single Man*, and the last two acts of *Outcast* his sense of reality frequently deserted him. There remain, however, four plays, *Mrs. Gorringe's Necklace*, *Cousin Kate*, *The Mollusc*, and *Captain Drew on Leave*, that contain so much of the real Davies that they must surely endure in the line of great English comedy so long as the English stage endures at all. The best scenes in these plays, the second act of *Cousin Kate*, the whole of *The Mollusc*, the second act of *Mrs. Gorringe*, and the second act of Captain Drew, remind us more definitely of the art of Jane Austen than of any other writer. That great lady would beyond any question have delighted in Mrs. Gorringe, in Mrs. Baxter and Mr. Baxter from *The Mollusc*, in *Cousin Kate*, first sister to Elizabeth Bennet, and in Miss Mills, the amorous spinster of *Captain Drew*. It is indeed astonishing to notice how little time has changed these types, how English these types are, and how admirably they are suited to the friendly, satirical spirit that belonged to the creator of Mrs. Baxter just as surely as to the chronicler of Miss Bates. And here one may notice a very remarkable characteristic of these Davies plays, that they more perhaps than any other plays in the English language do what good novels do—make us speculate on the lives of the characters in them before and after the action that we have been shown. Does anyone in the world believe in the existence of Paula Tanqueray or of Mrs. Dane or of Lady Windermere after the fall of the curtain? St. John Hankin indeed created people who lived beyond the action of the play, but his touch was so much more bitter than Davies's that we do not feel any affection for his people; but *Cousin Kate*, Mrs. Moxon of *Captain Drew*, the little typist in *A Single Man*, the poor heroine of *Outcast*, are our friends

◆ Afterword

even as Elizabeth Bennet, Emma Woodhouse, and David Copperfield are our friends. Davies himself loves them and as he develops them he has that sense of discovery about them that belongs always to the true creative artist. Without making any odious comparison, this can be seen very clearly when one compares *The Mollusc* with a play like *The Tyranny of Tears* by the late Mr. Haddon Chambers, the theme of the two plays being almost identical. Clever though *The Tyranny of Tears* is, it is a play of the theatre and its characters are theatrical puppets. But Mrs. Baxter goes gloriously on, far into time, triumphantly conscious that she will get her way so long as there is a man in the world, a way that no votes for women can affect so long as human nature remains unchanged.

It is interesting to speculate on the probable development of Davies's work had he lived. He was tending, as I have already said, towards more serious themes and a deeper presentation of life. The first act of *Outcast* shows that he was justified of his ambition, but artists are given only one of two things to do supremely well, and although I believe that he would have seen more and more clearly the way to blend plot with character and comedy with drama, we have definitely here in these two volumes the real essence of his art. One wonders sometimes when one goes to the theatre of today and sees so many plays false to life, lacking in all the true genius of the theatre, how long it will be before *Cousin Kate*, *The Mollusc*, and *Captain Drew* will delight us once again. That they will be delighting theatergoers of a hundred years from now is my own implicit belief.

OTHER BOOKS BY VERTVOLTA PRESS

———————————

THE MERCURIAN: THREE TALES OF ERIC JOHN STARK by Leigh Brackett
ebook: 978-1-60944-137-1

NIGHT OF THE LONG KNIVES by Fritz Leiber
print: 978-1-60944-112-8, $9.99
ebook: 978-1-60944-115-9

A CHRISTMAS CAROL by Charles Dickens
print: *978-1-60944-093-0, $9.99*
ebook: 978-1-60944-134-0

OLIVER TWIST: OR, THE PARISH BOY'S PROGRESS by Charles Dickens
print: 978-1-60944-092-3 , *$16.99*
ebook: 978-1-60944-133-3

ANARCHISM AND OTHER ESSAYS, by Emma Goldman
print: 978-1-60944-113-5, *$14.00*
ebook: 978-1-60944-114-2

VANCOUVER'S DISCOVERY OF PUGET SOUND: *Portraits and Biographies of the Men Honored in the Naming of Geographic Features of Northwestern America*, by Edmond S. Meany
978-1-60944-126-5, *$16.99*

D'ORCY'S AIRSHIP MANUAL: *An International Register of Airships With A Compendium of the Airship's Elementary Mechanics*, by Baron Ladislas D'Orcy
978-1-60944-126-5, *$19.95*

vertvoltapress.com

www.ingramcontent.com/pod-product-compliance
Lightning Source LLC
Chambersburg PA
CBHW060526080526
44586CB00012B/635